It's Not What You Eat,
It's Why You Eat It

To my wife Josephine who never ceases to encourage
and love me

To Henry and Hannah for their unconditional love

To Peter and Annabel for their guidance and example

It's Not What You Eat, It's Why You Eat It

The successful way to overcome eating problems

Beechy Colclough

VERMILION
London

First published in 1995

1 3 5 7 9 10 8 6 4 2

Text copyright © Beauchamp Owen Colclough 1995
Foreword copyright © Elton John

Beauchamp Owen Colclough has asserted his moral right to
be identified as the author of this work in accordance with
the Copyright, Design and Patents Act 1988.

First published in the United Kingdom in 1995 by Vermilion
an imprint of Ebury Press
Random House UK Ltd
Random House
20 Vauxhall Bridge Road
London SW1V 2SA

Random House Australia (Pty) Ltd
20 Alfred Street, Milsons Point, Sydney,
New South Wales 2061, Australia

Random House New Zealand Limited
18 Poland Rd, Glenfield,
Aukland 10, New Zealand

Random House, South Africa (Pty) Limited
PO Box 337, Bergvlei, South Africa

Random House UK Limited Reg. No. 954009

A CIP catalogue record for this book is available from the
British Library.

ISBN 0 09 179126 X

Typeset by SX Composing, Rayleigh, Essex
Printed and bound in Great Britain by Mackays of Chatham

Papers used by Vermilion are natural, recyclable products
made from wood grown in sustainable forests.

Contents

Acknowledgements

With thanks:

To Fiona Bowen, Dietician, BSc, SRD for her kind assistance with the key nutritional points on pages 52, 53, 54 and 55

To all the people I have worked with who have courageously shared their experiences with me

To all the therapists, doctors and psychiatrists I have worked with throughout the world and the self-help group members all of whom have so openly shared their knowledge and ideas with me

To Josephine for the major contribution she has made in the writing of this book

Beechy
March, 1995

Foreword
by Elton John

I entered a re-habilitation clinic in 1990 for drug addiction, alcoholism and bulimia. Of the three addictions I had no idea that my compulsive over-eating, bulimia, was the most severe. To me I was a drug addict and an alcoholic, the food was just a by-product.

Although my doctor had pointed out to me that food was my number one drug of choice, I was very sceptical about this. Even though throughout the whole of my life, even when I was a kid, I had had trouble with my weight. I binged on food, I put on weight easily, I tried so many diets to control my weight; I eventually became bulimic, completely ignorant of what that does to one's weight and to one's self-esteem. It was only when I started writing some stuff in re-hab and getting honest that I found, hey, my doctor was right all along.

Looking back over my life I see that I was never really taught how to eat. We use food for solace, for gluttony, for celebration. Before I became an alcoholic and drug addict I used food when I was miserable, when I was happy and this would have carried on for the rest of my life until I faced up to it and became a wiser man.

I treat food now with the utmost respect. I am so glad that I did find out that I was a compulsive over-eater, it has helped me so much with my recovery from my other addictions. And I eat very well, I don't starve and I don't miss out on anything. It's not easy, sometimes I am good, sometimes I am not good. I do not eat sugar and I try to stay away from white flour. That is never always easy but, for me, cutting the sugar out was a big, big help.

I must point out that Beechys book is not recommending a diet. When I first went into re-hab I only lost one and one half pounds in five weeks, but my body shape changed enormously. I was very angry about this but they said, listen Elton, this is not a diet, this is not a fad for three months, we are teaching you how to eat for the rest of your life and we are teaching you how to eat sensibly. We are teaching you how to respect food and to not let food have a hold on you.

So that's the way it is for me, not a day goes by when I don't think about my food, when I'm not careful, and my life has changed dramatically. I am a much happier person as a result of knowing and respecting food and food disorders.

So many people, especially men, are ignorant about food disorders. It is something that they don't talk about, it is especially something that the British aren't very good at talking abut. My advice to anybody who has always had a problem with food is to sit down and write how you have eaten throughout your life, take it to a GP or a nutritionist and ask them to give you some help now.

Food for me is all about maintaining my recovery, it is the most important process of my recovery. I hardly ever think about my drug addiction or my alcohol abuse. And I'm very proud of my recovery, it's the hardest thing that I have ever had to do.

I welcome Beachy's book on eating disorders because it explains to people who have an eating problem that their abuse of food can be changed.

So, get honest, get real and own up to – it's not what you eat it's why you eat it.

Elton John
February, 1995

Introduction

I really hope that you will find this book helpful. I have written it especially for those of you who know, deep down inside, that there is something wrong and that, time and time again, the only solution to it seems to be dieting, exercising or purging, so food is never allowed to take its rightful place in your life.

Over the years that I have worked with men and women with eating problems, I have learnt one important lesson from them: for these people it is *not* what they eat but *why* they eat it, or avoid eating it. It all comes down to feelings. Food can suppress feelings and starvation creates numbness.

So you see this is why this book contains *no* diet or weight chart. What I hope you will find is practical advice about managing your food and helpful strategies to assist you to look at what is really going on, so that you don't have to carry on with something that so obviously does not work for you.

I want the programme in this book to treat you as the special individual that you are. You may need medical advice or you may need to visit a nutritionist, but I urge you to talk through your own individual requirements and bear in mind the suggestions I have made in the food plan. I want you to know that my approach is to treat you as a person and not to tell you what you should look like – our society does enough of that. All I will strongly maintain is that your weight should be *medically* acceptable. Let's face it, if you are so thin that your menstrual cycle has stopped, you can't sit on a hard chair because your bones protrude, or you are so overweight that you become breathless and have high blood pressure –

then what are you doing to yourself? That is what concerns me. You need to be able to live life unhindered by unnecessary medical problems and, more than that, you need to feel good about yourself. What you look like is only part of that.

This book will ask you to look again and again into yourself – not at your plate. So, remember, this is not a diet book. This is a book which, I hope, will set you free from diets. You need to be able to make changes and stick with them – not go on a diet because, at the end, people like you always give up diets.

Let me explain a little more of what I mean. I would imagine, if you are reading this book, that some of you will be doing so for what may seem like, on the surface, a variety of different problems. But, as you continue to read on, you will realize the striking similarities.

I hope that this book will help both men and women who may be:

1. Overweight and stuck in compulsive overeating;

2. Overweight and ruled by diets, weight loss and immediate weight gain;

3. Bulimic;

4. Anorexic;

5. Those with a 'perfect figure', yet are not satisfied, who constantly feel driven to exercise and 'healthy' eating.

So, what will you all have in common? Plenty. I would imagine that if you are reading this book it will be because you are stuck in what I see as the Weight War. Just as in any real battle, it is important to be able to identify the enemy and understand what it is that you are fighting. Tragically, most people end up fighting themselves. The purpose of this book is to help you look again at what is really happening and to help you begin to tackle this problem from a very different angle.

When you move on to the opening chapters I hope that

you will begin to be able to identify yourselves more fully. Meanwhile, let us begin to look again at the real nature of these problems and the diverse experiences that I know you will have been having, as well as some of the questions that you have been asking:

1. What is the matter with me? I promised that I would lose weight and I have been dieting for a couple of days and now I just can't keep it up?

2. I keep promising myself that I will get around to dieting, but I can't even make a start. What is the matter with me that I just keep eating and eating? I have even reached a point where I am eating in secret places because I just don't want people to know how much I am really eating. I wonder if there is anyone else like me? I feel like a freak.

3. I am so disgusted with myself. I eat and eat. If anyone knew how much they would be horrified. I reach a point where I can hardly breathe, then I make myself sick. I get so frightened though. It is so out of control. I keep saying that I will never do it again but I can't stop. Is there really any hope for me?

4. I can clearly remember feeling so good when the weight started to come off. I had been bingeing before and, all of a sudden, I just found this miraculous diet. Then I just started to cut back, more and more. I also vomited even when I had hardly eaten. I started to feel so powerful and that I could conquer anything.

    Now I feel lost and just can't let myself eat, and I know that there is something really wrong, but I don't know how to break this. Will I ever be that happy person I was before all this started to happen? People call me attention-seeking and I get angry. I wish I could tell someone how I really feel.

5. All my friends are jealous of me. My stomach is so flat. Little do they know how I torture myself. If I eat anything

I really enjoy I feel so guilty. I don't have to use vomiting, dieting or laxatives because I hardly ever eat too much anyway, but I feel so bad about myself and feel so trapped. I wonder if anyone else can understand that I am unhappy?

6. I used to be really plump at school and was really teased. When I got to my teens I started to diet, and I felt stupid because boys shouldn't have to do this. Then I got into doing a lot of weight training and running and now I am just obsessed. Do you know that I am no happier than when I was that podgy teenager? What is really the matter with me? Everyone says that I look great, but it hasn't made me feel any different.

I think that you will begin to imagine that these extracts have come from people who will 'look' very different, and the quantities of food that they eat will be different; but there are some very striking similarities, particularly:

Dissatisfaction

Unhappiness

Feeling that there is something wrong

Food/starving/exercise are used as 'medicators'

Low self-esteem

Lack of confidence

These people have what I call 'eating disorders'

Some of you may have achieved the 'perfect' figure, but the startling reality is that your situation is not necessarily different because losing the weight has not solved whatever is really wrong, and that is why so many people go back to gaining weight.

Food is not the enemy, in fact for many people it becomes like a friend who will, of course, eventually betray them. What people do with food is the problem, and it is so often used to 'medicate' feelings. You will often hear the average person in the street say, 'I felt really fed up so I decided to buy myself a box of chocolates as a treat.' For those of you with eating disorders this type of action can never be controlled. Just as there are some people who cannot control their consumption of alcohol.

What I would like you to do, before you continue any further, is just stop and think how you would describe your particular problem. Please be honest with yourself – this is something that is for you only – you don't have to show it to anyone else.

Please write it down.

One thing that is so important is to understand that there is no magic answer. It is also important to be realistic and remember that if you want things to be different, you will have to start to do something different. THIS DOES NOT MEAN GOING ON A DIET. If you go on a diet it means that at some stage the diet will stop and this is the problem. Whatever you do I want you to be able to sustain it, and also understand that we need to look at why this has been happening, and why you have been using food in this way.

If you are really being honest, what do you think needs to change with your eating habits?
What do you say to yourself about why this happens? What is going on?

Please keep these answers as we need to refer back to them.

When you are ready, I also want you to get a recent photograph of yourself and keep it for an exercise we will do later on in the book.

You can if you want to

It is so important to believe that, bit by bit, this time can be different. You know from previous experiences what changes you need to make. All your previous efforts have not gone to waste, they are really valuable clues as to what needs to be done differently this time. So it's not as if all the diets, different food plans, different food combinations and calorie counting have been failures, remember you were only doing the best you could and what you knew how to do. It doesn't necessarily mean that they were wrong, and the wonderful thing about what I am suggesting is that you only have to do it one day at a time. You only have to live one day at a time, you can't live two days or a week at a time, just twenty-four hours a day.

Now you have probably heard this expression before – but, believe me, it is true: 'All you have to do is concentrate and focus on today because today is all we've got.' You can make plans for the future and project all sorts of things, but the reality is that you've only got today. Now you know what is going to happen tomorrow, I will be your manager and your agent and you and I will make a fortune! But the truth is that we don't know what's going to happen tomorrow, so doesn't it make sense just to live today? Really work hard on understanding this concept because this is going to be so important in your recovery from your eating disorder.

Can you remember the last diet you went on? On the very first day you'd be thinking what you'd be like in ten days' or two weeks' time? You are always thinking ahead, you never keep things to the same day. Well this time it is going to be different. I'd like you to take a little bit of time and think back over the last four diets, or times that you've tried very hard to lose weight. Can you do this for me? Think about this very carefully. Have an honest look at what happened.

Now I know that for each one of you reading this book your circumstances are different, but I think there are some similarities. One of these is that you are totally obsessed with eating when you are not eating. What I mean is that you build yourself up so much with your diet that you become totally obsessed with not eating. This mode of thinking can go into reverse when this happens and then all you really want to do is eat. So, have a look at how long you've lasted on your diet when you've been thinking like that.

Another sure-fire way to fail is to miss meals. Maybe not taking breakfast, skipping lunch, just having breakfast and an evening meal, or maybe not eating all day until the evening. What happens then is that you become increasingly hungry and once you start eating, you can't stop. Another way of setting yourself up for failure is by comparing yourself to other people, particularly if you've been dieting with them, or if you've joined a slimming club where you compare yourself with other people every week. If they've done better than you, you'll feel that you haven't succeeded enough and you'll come away from the meeting feeling like a failure – so you start to beat yourself up and then go back to the food.

As far as I'm concerned, the main reason why you easily fail with your dieting is because all you think about is food. You are actually convinced that the only reason you are overweight is because of food, but the reality is that it is because of your feelings that you overeat. Your feelings determine everything that you do. If you're feeling good about yourself, achieving things and feeling happy, the last thing that you'll do is overeat. You will not be bad to yourself or punish yourself in this way. You'll want to maintain that good feeling. Everyone wants to feel good, but the trap that the compulsive overeater falls into is that s/he thinks that food will make her/him feel better – but that sensation is short lived because you feel bloated and disgusted. You'll increase your weight, and you'll feel out of control, worthless, useless and not a part of anything. Oh yes, food will make you feel something, but it won't be anything positive. It will be negative. Overeating, undereating, vomiting or purging will take away all your choices and all your potential. Yes, you have potential. You just haven't given yourself a chance to develop it because you can't function properly while you are using food to medicate your feelings.

You have no chance of thinking straight, making good decisions, giving clear directives, concentrating properly, or working to your full potential. You just can't do it. You know it and I know it, so let's not get into a squabble about this. I am telling you quite directly that you have unused potential. You've an abundance of it – and you will see this if you will just start to look after yourself. Ask yourself these questions:

> ❛ Is this good enough? Is this all I'm worth? Is this the way it's going to stay? ❜

The answer is frankly, 'YES' everything will stay the same unless you do something about this. Only you can take the initiative. Only you can make the decision. Only you can really make up your mind that something is going to happen and that you will start to look at your eating disorder and in turn reap the benefits of your potential.

Now you can say to me, 'I've never had any potential. I've never been good at anything. I've never been able to finish anything I've started. I always but-out half-way through. I can't concentrate on anything. I'm doing two or three things at a time.' But again ask yourself, 'How much had you made up your mind to do something rather than try to do it?' In the past have you genuinely made up your mind that you were going to succeed at something? Finish it and make a good job of it? How much commitment have you put into things that you've tried in the past? It wouldn't surprise me if you make up your mind before you even start that you aren't going to make a good job of it, and that it isn't worth doing because you'll fail anyway. I'm not having a go at you or being cheeky, I'm just being really honest – because this type of negative thinking has got to stop. How much unhappiness do you want?

You can make the decision right now. You can tell yourself that you have the potential to recover from the situation that you're in at the moment, and that you can start to move your energy into getting better. If you just put a quarter of the energy that you've been using for your eating disorder, into getting better, you will see positive results.

Before you start to think about your unused potential, let's just look at the different levels that you're going to be working on to help yourself move from the negative place that you're in – because until you do this, you won't be able to feel or see clearly the potential that you have.

The six levels of recovery

Feeling or emotional level

By not overeating you will gain the ability to feel and express feelings. At the start this may be frightening and you may find that people will see you angry, so you've got to learn the difference between asserting yourself and being angry. In the past you've shown anger because you've been caught out or confronted about you behaviour and you haven't been able to tell the truth, so you've got very angry. Allowing yourself the ability to feel and express your feelings honestly is a very positive step in your recovery.

Physical level

Start to respect your body by eating properly and healthily. Personal hygiene is important. I'm not saying that you haven't had good personal hygiene, but some of you know that you've let yourself go in different areas, and it is something that you'll really want to get back as part of your self-respect. Clothes are important to you too and once you start to lose some of the excess weight, or maybe gain some weight, you'll want to start looking nice again. When you feel good on the inside you will want to look good on the outside. That is the difference, you'll be getting better from the inside out. Many people dress themselves up and paint their faces, and to the outside world they look good – but really inside they are in turmoil. So what we are talking about is you getting better from the inside out.

Mental level

Working on your ability to grow – physically, mentally and

spiritually – and to make changes that you thought were never possible – changes that you thought other people could make but not you. Start to read more and take notice of the things going on around you. Mentally stimulate yourself, because remember you've been numbing your feelings for such a long time with food.

Social level

The ability to develop and maintain meaningful relationships. You may find this very difficult to start with because you will have had difficulty having a relationship with yourself, never mind anybody else, so this will have to be taken slowly and very gently. Remember you are going to be very vulnerable, as you stop medicating with food. Your feelings are going to be right out there and you are going to be very sensitive. So you've got to protect yourself and not rush into things too easily. Don't say yes to everything just because all of a sudden you are being noticed. Remember you are a very important person. You are worth an awful lot. I know that, at the moment, you don't feel as if you are, but you are, and we are going to get to the point where you will say, 'Yes, I'm OK – I am worth something – I am worth loving and I do have a right to be treated properly and with respect.' But to start with you've got to learn to treat yourself with respect so remember that, 'To love and be loved are basic and necessary needs for you'.

Spiritual level

I find that a lot of people I talk to want to confuse spirituality with religion. Spirituality and religion are worlds apart. Spirituality is all around you, wherever you are at this very moment, there is something spiritual very close to you. You could be reading this book in the garden. Look at the garden, see how peaceful it is, or maybe you are looking out on to fields, or on an aeroplane. Look out of the window and see the beauty of the clouds in the sky. Maybe you are in a room that you like where you feel safe. Spirituality is a feeling, it's a sense of goodness and well-being and we all have that inside us. Maybe you're wearing a piece of jewellery that someone very close to you has given you. Touch it, feel it, and get a sense of goodness from it. Think of the person who gave it to you. Isn't that a good feeling? That is what spirituality is – a goodness, and you have that goodness inside you. It's going to be very important for you to develop that goodness and turn it into spiritual strength that will help you live a day at a time. Someone once said to me: 'Religion is for people who are frightened of going to hell, and spirituality is for those of us who have been there'. I really believe the truth in this. Look at the hell you've been in or are in at the moment. Think of the relief and the peace of mind that you're going to get on a daily basis as you come out of that hell. But you are going to need these six levels to help you recover.

Last, but not least:

Level of will

The will to recover. The will to live. The will to find yourself. The will to face you fear and go beyond it. The will to take risks. The will to look at yourself in the mirror and say, 'I deserve a chance. I deserve to get better'. I promise you that if you work at these levels and start to look after yourself, you will feel good beyond your wildest dreams. Now I'm not talking about money, or presents or success, etc., although having said that you probably will get a lot of them. Really what I'm talking about is that inner feeling of peace – a happiness that you have never really experienced – a happiness that you can't buy. It's priceless and it's just waiting on you if you will take responsibility for yourself and take your first step into recovery. As I write in Chapter 4, food needs to take its rightful place in your life, because you need to eat to live not live to eat, and you need to be able to manage your food rather than be managed by it. I know that you can do this if you want to. It's no good putting it off any longer, you've been putting it off for long enough. The time to start is now. Whether you are reading this book in the morning, afternoon or the middle of the night – I don't care! I need you to make your decision now and say to yourself, 'Enough is enough. I'm sick and tired of being sick and tired.' I know that you can do this – I have no doubts – but me believing this is no good if you don't.

So you've got to make your mind up, start trusting and accept that you don't know everything. You've got to accept that the way you've been doing things is not the way to get better. You've got to accept that you need help and that it's not going to be easy, and if you really want recovery you're going to have to go to any lengths to get it. This isn't an audition – you've already got the part. I'm not talking about someone else's reality – I'm talking about yours. There is only you and me here. I don't see anyone else. So it's time to get honest and real or stay as you are, stay with what you've got. If this is the case then it's pointless you reading any more of this book, maybe the best thing to do is give it to someone else who really wants the recovery. I hope you make the right decision. You can if you want to.

Self-Assessment assignment

Please answer the following with specific examples. Each example should state:

(a) Where and when the situation happened.
(b) Who else was involved.
(c) What your behaviour was like.
(d) What you were eating at the time (really think about the quantities). Give at least two or three specific examples.

Section I – Compulsiveness

This section will help you explore just who is in control. Do you really believe it is you?

In what ways has your overeating, starving or inducing vomiting led to any of the situations detailed below?

1. Accidents or dangerous situations (to myself and others).
2. Preoccupation with food.
3. Attempts to control my eating.
4. Loss of control of my eating and my behaviour.

Section II – Chaos

How has my inability to control my use of food, my behaviour and my feelings, affected the following?

1. My family and social life.
2. My spiritual life (i.e. values, principles, beliefs, self respect).
3. My work and financial life.
4. My health.

1
Yes, you! – Recognizing and identifying the problem

Reading a book like this tells me that there is a part of you that knows you need to do something different. There will also be the side of you that doesn't want to let go, or feels that it isn't possible. This is all part of the Weight War, part of the struggle; but believe me you can strengthen the side of you that wants to and needs to change.

What often blocks people from moving on and changing is simply not really identifying *what the problem is*, and if you don't really see the problem how can you see the solution when it is within your grasp?

Let me illustrate what I mean using this fable I heard at a conference several years ago.

6 There was a priest who lived in a beautiful English village close to a river. One day it started to rain, and it poured and it poured and poured for several days until the river broke its bank and flooded the village. The priest's devoted parishioners found a boat, rowed towards his house and found him sitting on the kitchen table with three feet of water below him. They shouted, 'Quickly we have a boat, wade out to us and we will take you to safety.' 'No,' he replied – 'I'm safe and well, the Lord will look after me.' So they rowed away.

The next day the level of the flood rose and the parishioners came again in the boat, fearing for him, but again he told them to leave and that his Lord would protect him.

The following day the parishioners looked out of their windows and saw that the level of the water had risen even more. The three of them got into their boat and rowed to the priest's house. By this time the priest was sitting on the roof, hanging on to the chimney, looking somewhat perplexed. They shouted up to him, but again he told them to go away.

The next day the water rose again and the priest drowned. He arrived in Heaven and promptly made an appointment to see God. He knocked on his office door and entered somewhat in a rage.

'Hello,' said God, 'How are you?'

'Well, to be perfectly honest, Lord, I am somewhat upset. I have spent years doing your work on earth and I feel that you let me down when you allowed me to drown like that. I would have thought that you of all people would have helped me.'

'That's a bit rich, isn't it?' said God. 'After all, I sent a boat to get you three times and would you get in it? No you wouldn't. You just kept taking things into your own hands . . .' **,**

You see, I know that when you are desperate it is hard to see the solution, and it is hard to see the answers. We all have 'pictures' of what the solution should be, so when we busily seek it, we miss the real solution just because it isn't always what we think it should be. In the strongest terms – IF YOU KNEW THE SOLUTION, YOU WOULDN'T BE READING THIS BOOK. So, please, join forces with me as we look again.

So many people ask me for definitions of these problems. Later on I will provide a simple and straightforward questionnaire; but before we do this let's first look at the different guises of these problems:

Compulsive overeating

There will be some of you who have been overeating for a long time and I know that you end up 'wearing' your problem. (If you are *truly* content with your weight then this is a different issue). If you are not, read on.

So many of you desperately hide the amounts that you are

eating and are forced to eat secretly, often shopping in different supermarkets to hide the amounts you are buying. Others will be loudly complaining, 'Yet another dinner party' or 'Another children's birthday party', when the only guest is you. Then there will be the fear and the questioning, 'Why do I continue to do this when I feel so bad? Another part of you will be saying, 'What's the point, I'm stuck like this.'

For anyone who is very overweight their goal should be to lose weight slowly. To reach a *medically acceptable weight*. I am not telling you to lose weight and then everything will be different. Although, having said that, I know that the world tends to treat overweight people in a disrespectful way; and that when you are very overweight you have a physical struggle. I know how much you fear sitting on a delicate chair in case it breaks, or you get stuck.

The nightmare of buying clothes – walking distances – the agony of twisting your ankle – the pains in your knees. So that burden needs to be released .It is so important for you to emerge from your weight. Come out from where you have been hiding.

Get a recent photograph of yourself and look at it. Ask yourself the most important question: 'Who does this weight belong to? Is it mine? Is it my mother's? Is it my father's? Why have I collected this? What is all this pain?' If you are having difficulty understanding what I am saying, make a list of five things that feel wonderful about the photograph . . . Now do you understand? Now can you see what food had done to you?

There is a war on – it's called the Weight War – and *you* are going to win it. You are going to get your independence, from the nightmare to the happiness that you deserve.

I know you will also be asking, 'Why did all this start?' 'Why me?' The answers can be so different that some people get scared; scared that something dark may have happened, or that they have no right to this problem because to all intents and purposes everything was OK in their past. The most important thing is to look at what was happening in your life before the overeating really began, and to make the decision today to get back in charge of the food by realising that it is *too powerful* to play around with. It needs to be cornered and put in its rightful place. You will never beat it until you stop the overeating. It needs to *stop*.

Dieting and overeating

I know how desperate you get. 'Yes, this time I've cracked it.' Your confidence increases. Everyone is saying how marvellous you look, then it all starts again. It's as if a green light comes on and you are helpless to stop what you know will inevitably happen. Each week the weight piles back on. Then you may regain a bit of control until the overeating starts again. Then you feel 'What's the point', and all the small-size clothes are put away until the next time.

You know how important it is not to let that green light come back on. Once you have given yourself permission it's as if the food comes marching back in, and there it is back in charge of your life. You don't take the food. It takes you.

Bulimia

This term is used more and more to describe those of you who use vomiting, laxatives and overexercise to control your weight. Sometimes you will binge, sometimes not, but as time goes on the purging gets out of control.

I know how much you hate this behaviour and the self-loathing and self-disgust it involves. At first it seemed the perfect solution. 'Yes,' you thought, 'I can eat whatever I want and I can stay slim'. But the important question is why do you *need* to eat so much? Why do you have to convince yourself that the 'perfect solution' is to torture yourself with vomiting and laxative abuse? So many people have told me the anguish and the rituals involved. The pain of thrusting fingers into the throat, and the agony of resorting to other objects when that no longer works. What about the excruciating pain involved when you've taken laxatives; and the shame when you can't get to the toilet in time? This is torture. I know that there will also be that side of you that feels 'in control' and powerful. You need to ask yourself, at what cost?

Ask yourself another important question, 'What has been happening to trigger this behaviour?' You know, as well as I do, that this is such a violent way to treat yourself. What has happened to make you value yourself so little? What is wrong that makes you feel bad about yourself? Please don't be afraid that I am hinting at sexual abuse. Yes, some of you may have been abused, but for others there are different reasons, and those reasons are valid.

Anorexia

People become anorexic in different ways. You may once have been overweight or you may have had what everyone else saw as the perfect figure. But, for whatever reason, you have gone 'on strike' about food. Don't you just get sick of being told to eat, and all the focus being on weight gain? Someone needs to ask you what this is all about and, yes, you might feel that you need to talk to someone outside the family.

You may be using vomiting, laxatives or exercise to control the weight, or you may simply be drastically reducing your food intake. Isn't it painful when you can't even bear to drink a nil calorie glass of water because a full bladder feels so strange and bloated?

Anorexia is a frightening problem, especially for you. What once made you feel so 'in control' and confident turns against you so that even when you are dying to eat, you just can't let yourself, or you chew a little corner of something and spit it out. I'm not going to suggest that you have to regain lots of weight quickly, but that you have to accept the need to eat and live, and accept that there is another way of resolving whatever it is that is troubling you so much. You know, deep down inside, that you need to do something different. Don't delay that decision. Do it today, and take it a day at a time.

Trapped in the perfect figure

You are the one with the 'hidden' problem. No one would ever really guess. You are careful with what you eat (at least in public). Yes, if you overdo it, you may take laxatives or be sick, but often you just control yourself. Remember, I'm not talking about someone who is feeling good about themselves. I'm talking about you and about how that 'perfect' exterior is simply a facade behind which you hide feelings of loathing and self-doubt. (Although it helps when you pat your hand over that very flat stomach.)

Now that you have read this far, I'd like you to make a promise to yourself: that you'll continue on to the end of the book. If it helps you, don't tell anyone what you are doing (other than your doctor).

I'm sure you are also thinking again about the food plan. Please stop dwelling on any fears of deprivations. 'What no sugar!!' I have yet to meet anyone with an eating disorder who can just manage 'one chocolate'. Believe me you aren't stopping anything. You are about to start something very positive.

Let's now look at some behaviours, experiences and symptoms that characterize these various problems. Remember, as you read these, the degree of your problem may vary and the most important thing to do if you are concerned is to speak to your GP.

Recognition of bulimia and of bulimics who use purging

This involves eating 'binges', rapid eating and eating in

secret. There will be feelings of loss of control, the inability to stop binges and episodic binge eating. Those who suffer with this problem are aware that their eating habits are abnormal, and they are fearful of not being able to stop voluntarily. They often experience self-deprecating thoughts and depressed moods.

Signs

Preoccupation with food, eating and not eating.
Excessive concern about weight.
Strict dieting followed by eating binges (which can consist of up to 15,000 calories at a time).
Experiencing guilt and shame about amounts eaten.
Frequently overeating.
Being secretive about amounts eaten and use of vomiting/laxatives/enemas/diet pills/diuretics.
Anger if questioned about eating habits, or weight.
Feeling out of control.
If purging, will disappear after a meal, will look flushed afterwards, and will often have blood-shot eyes.
Mood swings.
Low self-esteem.

Physical signs

Menstrual cycle may be present, irregular or absent.
Brittle hair and nails.
Poor complexion.
Weight loss, weight gain.
Rarely particularly overweight.

Physical signs strongly associated with vomiting

Loss of tooth enamel.
Brittle hair and nails.
Self-harming.
Poor complexion.

Split lips, mouth sores.
Weight loss, weight gain.
Swollen glands.
Broken blood vessels.
Sore throat and associated croaky voice.

Medical concerns

Electrolyte imbalance
Haemorrhaging

Recognition of compulsive overeating

This involves eating, either constantly eating throughout the day or 'binges', rapid eating and eating in secret. There will be feelings of inability to control food intake and feelings of hopelessness and helplessness.

Signs

Can be a pattern of dieting followed by rapid weight gain.
Possible abuse or use of amphetamines, laxatives, enemas and diuretics.
Inability to maintain consistent weight.
Experiencing guilt and shame about amounts eaten.
Being secretive about amounts eaten.
Eating in secret and possibly eating at night.
Often denial about amounts eaten.
Anger if questioned about eating habits or weight.
Mood-swings.
Preoccupation with food.
Low self-esteem.
Less sexually active.
Compulsive spending.
Emphasis on being liked and accepted.

Physical signs

Obesity.
Possible periods of weight loss and weight gain.

Medical concerns

Degenerative joint disease.
Endocrine disorders.
Arthritis.
Pulmonary disease.

Recognition of anorexia nervosa

Involves a severe disturbance of body image and a refusal to maintain normal body weight.

Signs

Dieting when not overweight.
Claims 'feeling fat' when not overweight.
Preoccupation with food, calories, nutrition and/or food preparation.
Denial of hunger.
Excessive exercise, or simply not resting/restlessness.
Frequently weighing oneself.
Use of laxatives, and/or vomiting and/or dieting to control weight and/or diet pills or diuretics.
Disappearance after meals (if using vomiting or laxatives).
Hiding food/throwing it away/hoarding food.
Periods of bingeing.
Refusal to drink normal amounts of fluid.
Perfectionism.
Low self-esteem.

Physical signs

Extreme weight loss.
Loss or irregular menstrual cycle.
Poor complexion.
Brittle hair and nails.
Hair loss.
Lanugo (excessive body hair).
Leg cramps.
Feeling cold.
Interrupted sleep patterns.
Less sexually active/avoids sexual relationships.
Frequent headaches.

Medical concerns

Electrolyte imbalance
Haemorrhaging.
Starvation.
Dehydration.

2

It's your feelings, not the food

Getting to the root of the problem

Understanding anything is the key to success. This chapter explains how to understand why food has become the problem it is. Understanding means being honest with yourself. Please do the exercise at the end of the chapter *honestly*.

What do we do with our feelings? Where do they go? When we express feelings does that mean that we do not have them any more? That they are over and done with? Maybe we don't express our feelings, but bottle them up inside? Then what happens? Do we let other people deal with our feelings for us? Do we let them suggest that we feel a certain way just to agree with them because we don't want an argument or we don't want to upset them? We want them to like us and perhaps we don't want to tell them the way we really do feel. Maybe we're feeling shameful, isolated, remorseful, hurt, or sad; or maybe it's because we just can't trust people enough to tell them how we really feel.

Talking about feelings

This is a very difficult thing to do. For a start you are exposing yourself to the other person or persons involved. You are quite possibly going to say some things that may well upset other people. Maybe you have an overriding fear that if you do tell someone how you really feel about a situation, or indeed about the person themselves, they will disagree with you, and they will become upset or angry with you; so then what is going to happen? The little voice comes back in your head whispering, 'Don't say anything, just keep it to yourself,' and then they will keep liking you, they won't think badly of you'. But if you don't say anything, and you keep your feelings bottled up, what happens? Well, you know the answer to that question better than I do, you know how badly you feel about yourself when you don't express your inner feelings. Believe me, I know how hard it is to do this, I know that there is so much involved in expressing our feelings, because there is a lot at stake. Once we do start to talk about, and disclose how we are feeling, we are exposing ourselves. In lots of ways you are throwing yourself open to whoever the listener is, and you are not sure what they may do with these disclosures. I'm not talking about an everyday situation such as, 'Oh, good morning, how are you today?' answer 'Oh, I'm fine;' or the man who walks into the shop and says, 'Hello, Mrs James, how's everything at home?' Answer, 'Oh, it's OK, everything is great, the family is wonderful, the dog is fine, the cat's well behaved and the birds are singing.' Or, 'Hello, Mr Brown, how are you today?' Answer, 'Oh well, you know.' But if we are talking about feelings, what does all that talk really mean? Not a lot. Those types of disclosure or interactions were delivered in a very superficial way, and that is how people interact with each other, on a very superficial level. Good morning – good afternoon – good night – good evening – how are you? – lovely weather – shame about the weather – look at the price of this – gosh, things were different when I was younger – the youth of today – governments are all the same, etc, etc.

What I would like to discuss with you are our real feelings, our innermost feelings, our important feelings, the feelings that really change our moods. Have you ever been at work or at home or in some other situation and someone has said to you, 'Gosh you're really moody today, what's wrong?' What if the expression were changed to, 'Gosh you're feeling today'.

Imagine for a moment what that would feel like if someone said that to you, especially if they went on and said, 'You're really feeling today, why don't you talk to me about it?' What do you think your reaction would be? How do you think you would respond to the person? Would one of your reactions be, 'Don't be stupid, why are you talking to me like this? What's wrong with you?'

In most respects people don't talk about their feelings, they talk around them. It is much safer to do that, but in lots of ways for people like you and me, its more dishonest to do that because when we don't talk about our feelings we are left with all those feelings, and then what happens to us? Well the first thing that would probably happen is that if you aren't going to express how you feel, you will start to argue. Have you ever noticed what happens when people start arguing? Everyone speaks at once and no one listens; how can you listen when you are trying to get your point across? The same applies to the other person. When this situation happens, for people like you and me who have an abundance of feelings and who don't get a chance to express them or to talk them through, we medicate our feelings, and that is what you are doing with food; you are using food as the medicator for the way you are feeling. There are certain feelings that you don't want to talk about and you want to change them, so you'll eat something because by this time you probably would have learned that eating certain foods changes the way you feel. Food becomes a friend – it becomes a comfort – it becomes a vehicle that stops you looking at what is really happening to you. What really happens is that feelings don't change. What changes is the way we express our feelings.

Have you ever noticed what happens when you've been feeling angry? You've decided not to express the anger and you start to eat to stifle all the feelings that you are having. For a very short time this may feel as if it works for you as it seems to take away those feelings of anger, frustration, rage or, whatever it is you are experiencing; but the reality is that it doesn't. You end up feeling more angry than when you started, because you are still left with the feelings that you originally had. Then, when you have overeaten to a point when you feel so full up and you can't eat anymore, you feel disgusted with yourself, bloated and worthless. So instead of the food being any sort of a comfort it increasingly becomes your enemy. Then what happens is that your angry feelings come out in an unpleasant way. I don't believe for a minute that you've wanted to behave like that, but it's been taken out of your control because the feelings of disgust around the overeating have taken over, and the food is now in charge of your feelings and the way that you express them. It's like when you wake up first thing in the morning and the first thought that comes into your head is, 'Oh I didn't, did I? Oh God it must have been a bad dream,' but it wasn't. You'd like to think that you hadn't binged the night before, but the reality is that you have, and you are dreading seeing people because you feel overweight – you feel fat, you feel bloated – and you haven't slept well because you've been tossing and turning with all these feelings and thoughts going on in your mind.

When I talk to people about their feelings, I always use the term or analogy, 'a room inside'. Imagine a room inside ourselves where we keep our feelings. Now this might sound really silly, but bear with me for a minute. Just imagine that we store all our feelings in a room – all the feelings that we really don't want to talk about – all those dark thoughts; and we keep the door closed tightly. We are the only ones that have the key. We are the only ones who can open the door. Sometimes we go there on our own, and we go into that room and we look around, but you can't see much because it's dark, because those feelings are dark, and it's frightening because there are so many of them. All of a sudden you feel panicky, and you just want to get out of the room and shut the door tightly behind you.

Have you ever had anybody drop in on you unexpectedly, and your flat or your house or your apartment has been a bit untidy or messy. All of a sudden you panic, you'll lift up all the things that shouldn't be there and put them under the cushions, or put the newspapers underneath the carpet.

You'll put stuff behind the sofa and you'll run around trying to tidy things up really quickly. Well that's what we do with our feelings, we store them away and we forget that they exist. Sometimes you'll be feeling strange or moody, or feeling some thoughts of depression, but you won't really understand why. Well, it's because of all those unaddressed issues and all that stuff inside that we don't talk about or that we are frightened to even look at.

If you want to clear out a wardrobe or closet of all clothes, you have to look through them, you have to look at them, try them on and feel whether you want to keep them or whether you want to let them go. It's the same with our feelings, we have to look at them really closely, and look at whether they belong to us or not – whether those feelings of remorse, guilt, sadness and shame were given to us, or whether we really feel like that at all. This is very important and it is one of the major keys to freedom. There is nothing more important than looking at your feelings – your inner feelings – and understanding how they affect us, and how they can alter a mood. You may have not thought this way before and that's OK, why would you? Before I ever became aware of my alcoholism and my drug addiction, I just went about my day thinking that this was the way it was always going to be.

It wasn't until someone explained and pointed out to me that it was about my feelings – not the alcohol or the drugs – that I started to get well. This is what I'm saying to you – throughout this chapter – that it's not the food, it's your feelings, and the quickest way that you are going to recover from your food addiction is to look at your feelings, and how you may be using the food as a cushion for most of your emotional problems. Also how your overeating can distort those feelings.

Have you ever noticed how easy it is to become angry when you are eating? Think back for a moment and imagine what it's like to be on the receiving end of your anger. I would imagine that it is very threatening to the people that have to take this and also very hurtful. I'm not saying for one moment that you want to be threatening, or that you want to be hurtful, but it is what is happening to you because you are using the food to cope with your feelings instead of taking responsibility for the way you feel.

I talked earlier about how we want to change the way we feel. If you are constantly using food to do this, your feelings will become caught up in the pattern of behaviour that food causes. Try and grasp the concept that involving food doesn't help to make things clearer, it makes them more confused by distorting the situation. It distorts your perceptions and your rational thinking. It doesn't help you solve any of your problems, in fact it helps you to keep them. All that you are doing is adding eating problems to the situation, and naturally nothing is going to change. Everything is going to stay the same except for those few brief moments of reprieve you get. That is what food does, it gives you that short-term reprieve – numbs your feelings, numbs the worrying, numbs the fears, it numbs those feelings of inadequacy, of low self-worth, those feelings that you are not good enough. You sit and fantasize that everything is OK as you eat away at whatever is in front of you. Try and get a picture of this; try and get a picture of how sad this looks and how hopeless this situation is. It is imperative that you understand what is happening to you. You have to get a clear picture of this nightmare before you can actually take responsibility and say to yourself:

❛ I really want to do something about this. I want to change the way I'm living. I want to change my attitude to food. I want to manage food instead of being managed by it. I am a good person. I deserve this. I deserve a better life. I deserve to be happy. I deserve to live a happy day. To be good to myself. To be good to my husband. To be good to my wife. To be good to my children and to my friends, and the people around me who love me and have been there for me and have stayed loyal to me – even when I have behaved badly. Even when I have shouted at them for no good reason, or else sulked at them or have blamed them for the situations that haven't been their fault, when deep inside it's been me and my loneliness and my inadequacies and my deep unhappiness with myself that have driven me to behave like this. ❜

Understand that compulsive overeating, bulimia, anorexia and binge eating are illnesses. They are conditions. They are not normal things to do. Let yourself off the hook. You weren't supposed to know this – how would you? If you had of known that you were suffering from an illness, I am sure that you would have done something by now. But *now* is the time. It is time to say to yourself that you are going to take responsibility for your feelings – that you are going to face your feelings. You are not going to run away anymore. You are not going to run to the fridge. You are not going to run to the supermarket. You are not going to hide behind a cake, or endless bowls of cereal, or endless pieces of bread, or whatever trigger foods that you use to numb your feelings. Now is the time to take responsibility and to say to yourself that you are going to stand up and learn to be your own person.

Assignment

Let me give you something to do. Look at the list of feelings on the opposite page, and over the next month start to think about how you are feeling; become more aware of these feelings and start to identify how they affect you. If, for example, you are constantly tired, start to look at what you are doing, how physical are you being? How much running about are you doing? How much stress are you creating in your life? How angry are you? Yes angry.

I always see anger as the veil for other feelings. Look behind the anger, look at what is going on with you. This will really help you to see more clearly how you can deal with your feelings without using food. Look at the list of defences and do the same. Be scrupulously honest with yourself and look at your behaviour. Notice how you feel. Also be aware that the feelings don't have to be negative. If they are, there is another way out. That way is by facing them rather than eating on them and suppressing them.

Feelings

ABANDONED	ADVENTUROUS	AFRAID	ALONE
AMBIVALENT	ANGRY	ANXIOUS	ASHAMED
BEWILDERED	BORED	CALM	CARING
CHEATED	COLD	CONCERNED	CONFIDENT
COWARDLY	DEFEATED	DEFENSIVE	DEFICIENT
DISCOURAGED	DOWN	EAGER	ELATED
EMBARRASSED	ENERGISED	ENVIOUS	EXCITED
FAILURE	FEARFUL	FOOLISH	FRUSTRATED
GRATEFUL	GUILTY	HAPPY	HELPLESS
HESITANT	HOPELESS	HOSTILE	HURT
INFERIOR	IRRATIONAL	ISOLATED	JEALOUS
JOYFUL	KINDLY	LONELY	LOVING
MISERABLE	NATURAL	NERVOUS	NUMB
OVERCOME	OVERJOYED	PAINED	PEACEFUL
PIOUS	PLAYFUL	PLEASED	PROUD
PROVOKED	PUT OFF	PUT OUT	REFRESHED
REJECTED	RELUCTANT	REMORSEFUL	RESENTFUL
RESPECTFUL	SECURE	SELFISH	SELF-PITYING
STUBBORN	SUCCESSFUL	SUPERIOR	SUSPICIOUS
TIRED	TRANQUIL	TRAPPED	UNDERSTOOD
UNHAPPY	UNLOVED	UNSURE	UNWANTED
UNWORTHY	USED	WARM	WEARY

Defences

AGREEING	COMPLYING	CONFORMING	DISAGREEING
GENERALIZING	JUSTIFYING	LETHARGY	

Making excuses

'I DON'T KNOW'
'YES, BUT'
'I WILL WHEN I GET THE CHANCE'
'BUT YOU DON'T UNDERSTAND'
'IT'S NOT THAT EASY FOR ME'
'EVERYBODY DOES IT BETTER THAN I DO'
'I WOULD IF I COULD . . . BUT I CAN'T'

3

You are not the only one

'Other people suffer and I should know because I did too'

If I had a pound for every person who has walked into my office, sat down and made the following statement, I would be very rich:

> ❛ *I feel so lonely and isolated by the way that I eat.* How can I do something about this if you are the only person that I can talk to? Nobody seems to understand, or know how I am feeling, everybody just thinks that I'm fat and happy. But how can I tell them anyway – how can I tell them how much I eat. I can't tell them about the binges that I have, and how uncontrollable it feels – how once I start to eat I can't stop. It drives me to the point where I think I'm going crazy, and then I get so fed up with food that I literally just want to die – I just want to lie down and die because I can't take it anymore. For all the times I've said I'm going to quit and go on a diet, I always seem to go back to my old ways. Look at me, look how big I am. How can I tell anyone how I got this way when half the time I really don't know myself? And you Beechy, you don't have an eating disorder so how come you understand and say that you know how I'm feeling, how can you possibly know what it's like to start eating something and not being able to stop? ❜

Before I give an answer I usually sit quietly for a few moments and think about all the years that I spent *drinking and taking drugs,* and how I used to think that I was the only person who drank like I did, or who took pills like I did, or smoked dope like I did. For years and years, even though people close to me who I trusted had given me names and addresses of people to see, and who went out of their way to help me, I never believed for one moment that there was anyone else who actually felt the same way that I did. It probably sounds as if I'm being very big-headed to suggest that nobody else felt the same isolation, anger, remorse, guilt and loneliness that I felt. It would probably be more truthful to say that I just didn't take any notice of other people because I was so self-obsessed and totally self-centred that I was only interested in myself.

Another reason why I used to think that nobody else used alcohol and drugs like I did was because I never talked honestly about my feelings. I would never tell people how I really felt (why would I?) because for a long time I was convinced that I wasn't drinking too much. At certain times in my life, while I've been drinking or taking drugs, I've felt such total despair because I believed that no one would understand if I told them how I really felt. So, like you, I've had all those feelings.

The second part of my answer to the question 'How would you know what it felt like, Beechy?' would be to talk a little bit about a treatment centre I once worked at about eleven years ago. The treatment centre treated people with alcohol and drug problems only. I used to watch people when they first came in, and I noticed that certain things would happen to them. They would detox from their alcohol and drugs – and yes! they would come back to life and look very different. They'd have colour in their faces. However, I also used to notice what happened at meal times, and before meal times. These patients, for most of their lives, had never been interested in food and, all of a sudden, they would look forward to their meals. They would start buying a lot of sweets, chocolates and savouries, and then eventually they'd pretty much be eating all day. If they were smokers, their intake of nicotine would increase dramatically.

These people were medicating their feelings with food, and I started to observe this. I watched the mood changes at meal times, and the continual use of sugar throughout the day, and how patients would get 'high' by eating too much sugar; but because eating disorders were not really recognised in the treatment centre as any type of an addiction or illness, nothing was said. It was seen as healthy – 'Oh look, he's eating again, plenty of sweets, that's good his appetite's coming back.' Well, I started looking at it in a different way. I started seeing it as transferring the medicator, i.e. if they had been using alcohol, or drugs before, now they were using food, or sugar.

I talked about my thoughts on this to my colleagues, but they weren't really interested in my observations about the patients behaviour. Nonetheless, this didn't deter me from starting to learn about the way people medicate their feelings with food. I personally see no difference between alcohol addiction, drug addiction or food addiction. They are used for the same end – to medicate the way you feel – and they work! I don't have to tell you that.

I also very quickly learned that this is not only a women's illness as men suffer from compulsive overeating, undereating, anorexia or bulimia, just in the same way as women do. It never ceases to amaze me how people regard eating disorders as strictly a women's illness. This is totally untrue. I have treated many men with eating disorders. They feel exactly the same way as women. The same feelings of isolation, despair, loneliness and anger – the same feelings of low self-worth and low self-esteem, or the high achievers who never achieve enough for themselves. The anorexic male is doomed to control everything, but the reality is that everything is out of control. I find it sad that a lot of people want to look for the differences rather than the similarities between men and women who suffer from eating disorders.

It wasn't until I moved to another treatment facility that I actually started to treat people with eating disorders. I treated them in the same way as I'd been treating people with alcohol and drug problems, because I work on a 'feelings' level. I'm not interested in the alcohol, drugs or food – I'm interested in how you medicate the feelings that you have with whatever substance you are using. In this case we are talking about food.

Honesty about feelings

I have successfully treated countless people with eating disorders by using this method of therapy. It is very simple, there are no hidden deep therapeutic techniques. It is basically listening to what you are saying about how you feel, and giving you dignity and respect. It is about the way you feel, and if you're given a chance to express these feelings you will recover, but only if you start taking responsibility, and start getting really honest.

You must think about this for a moment. How many times have you honestly and openly talked to someone about your eating? Think about it – I would imagine not very often, or not at all. I understand this, I know how difficult it is, but you've got to make a start and come out of the wilderness, because you are not the only one. There are countless thousands of people who are suffering from the same problems and feeling the same feelings as you are, and you can find these people. You can connect with them. You can share with them and learn from them, and start to see light at the end of the tunnel – the tunnel that you thought would never end.

You are probably reading this and thinking, 'Oh my God, how will I even begin to talk about how I am feeling? Or how much I eat? Or the lies that I've told? Or the way that I've hidden food and denied what I'm doing?' I totally understand this, I know it's frightening to let someone in, but I also know that it's the only way out of this trap. You've got to make a start. You've really got to take the initiative and maybe for the first time in your career of overeating, undereating, etc. you will take responsibility and tell the truth.

Starting to get help

Let's just suppose for a moment that you're going to take my advice, and that you're actually going to do something. The first question is, 'Where can I go for help?' Now for me as a professional this is a very difficult question to answer because, unlike people with alcohol and drug problems, eating disorders are not so widely recognized everywhere. Some countries recognize these problems more than others but, for the most part, an eating disorder is not seen as a serious problem. I always advise people to go to their doctor first because people who have been abusing themselves with food may have caused themselves physical problems. Before you do anything about your eating disorder, whether you are starting an eating plan or considering any form of treatment, you must see your doctor. Go along and ask for his/her advice and hopefully he/she will have good information for you regarding your eating disorder. The doctor should be able to refer you to someone who can start you on the road to recovery.

Now I use the words 'good information' because I am well aware that there is a lot of bad information available. I have a professional obligation to give you the best help and advice that I can and to help you break free from this 'Hell' that you've been living in. This is only my personal opinion, but let's just have a quick look at what I would class as bad advice: 'Control yourself!' – 'Pull yourself together!' – 'Get yourself on a diet,' . . . etc. What sort of help is this? I mean, if you could control your eating you wouldn't be sitting having the conversation with this person, and you wouldn't be asking for help. You've already tried to control your eating, you've been trying to control it for years, but it doesn't work. As I've said repeatedly in this book: how do you control something that is out of control?

You and I aren't talking about social eating any more, or the sort of eating that everyone else is doing. We're talking about being dependent on food, structuring your whole day around food and about food controlling your life. We're talking about food getting in the way of everything that you've ever tried to achieve, food getting in the way of your relationships, and everyone that you come into contact with, and food totally isolating you from any sort of a normal life. So when you get the answer, 'Pull yourself together!' you are getting bad advice. It is what I call ignorance and a total lack of knowledge of eating disorders. If I sound angry, I am, because I think it is totally unprofessional for people in the medical profession not to have the right information to help people who suffer from this compulsive disorder.

In my professional opinion, the only way to recover from an eating disorder is abstinence. By this I don't mean to stop eating totally as you need food to live. What I mean is for you to manage your food instead of being managed by it. Abstinence from the foods that you overeat on is your key to freedom. However, managing the food is only one part of your recovery. Remember that you are still going to have those feelings to contend with. The feelings that you've been trying to suppress with the food, and all those other under-lining fears that you've been trying to quell with food will still be there. By seeking help, you will be taking the first step in the right direction. Start to talk about your feelings and get some help and understanding for yourself. This, in time, will help you to accept and come to terms with the issues that have been driving you in a very negative way.

Self-help groups

There are many self-help groups in existence today, who help people with eating disorders. One of the most success-ful groups that I am aware of is Overeaters Anonymous (OA). OA will work for you if you follow the very simple pro-gramme that they offer. There are OA meetings everywhere. Wherever you live there is an OA meeting place not too far away. If you want to know where they are, all you have to do is pick up the telephone. You will soon realize that you are not alone. There are thousands of people who feel like you and who have found a bridge to normal living.

Another important factor of the OA programme is that it is anonymous. You can go to meetings without worrying about who is going to talk about you, or how safe your exposed thoughts will be. You will be able to share your expe-riences, your strengths and your hope, and have the knowl-edge that they will stay in the room. You will feel a real sense

of freedom and safety at these meetings. The OA programme will help you get on with your life and at the same
time you will get support from people who understand.

Other forms of help

You may be someone who needs something more than a self-
help group. You may have come to a point in your addiction
where you need residential help. There are many hospitals,
treatment centres, and specialized clinics, that specifically
deal with people who have eating disorders. Some of these
treatment facilities will incorporate the OA programme into
their structure. In this sort of setting, you will be offered the
opportunity to look at your emotional, physical, mental, and
spiritual well-being. This type of treatment takes place
through group therapy, lectures, one-to-one counselling,
speciality groups, spirituality groups, relaxation techniques
and, most importantly, help to understand the OA programme.

One of the most important starting points is to come to
terms with understanding 'powerlessness' around food
which means that you will stop trying to control the uncon-
trollable.

The steps of the programme are simple and wonderfully
effective in helping you to arrest your behaviour. I cannot
emphasize enough the word 'arrest' for there is no cure for
the underlining condition. What I mean is that if you remain
abstinent from your trigger foods and eat three meals a day,
with nothing eaten between, you will be able to get on with
your life. But if you start to overeat, undereat, induce vomiting or take laxatives, you will be right back into the spiral of
your eating behaviour.

The treatment that I have used in helping people incor-
porates experiential therapy, through such things as educational lectures, psycho-drama, role playing, art therapy,
collages and intense group therapy. I like to look at the
patient's needs rather than the patient's wants. We all seem
to know what we want, but we very rarely take a look at what

we need. I also like to treat a person as a person rather than just an addict. Let me clarify that. Instead of saying, 'Here comes someone with a food, alcohol, exercise, sex problem, etc.', I say, 'Here comes a human being who is a very sensitive person' and we need to look at this person's needs and be able to formulate a suitable treatment plan for them, and for his/her family.

Above anything else you need a positive attitude that is going to be geared towards humour and happiness. You won't want to get well in an atmosphere of negativity, doom or gloom. My own personal philosophy is geared at looking at today, rather than repeatedly looking at yesterday. Yes, I do agree that we have to have a look back at the conse-quences and at what you've been doing with your life, but we don't have to stay there forever – we can work through the pain. I am always concerned when people come to me and say, 'I'm working on this issue'. What I want to say is, 'Why aren't you working through it instead of staying with the same old thing?'

It is time to start getting excited and motivated, to start believing that you have some choices in your life, and that you can have a future for yourself. If you choose, you can make some very positive changes rather than constantly dwelling on the failures and turmoil of your past. You can actually start believing that you will be able to cope rather than trying to escape all the time. I'm talking about self-dis-covery, dealing with people honestly, being open about your feelings, and taking responsibility instead of trying to escape.

If residential treatment does not suit you, or you have dif-ficulty affording this sort of help (it can be very expensive), there are many counsellors and therapists who will offer per-sonalized counselling or group therapy on an out-patient basis. A lot of these therapists will be offering men's, women's or mixed groups. There is a lot of help available out there, but you've got to make the decision that you want some help. All you have to do is pick up the phone, see your doctor and get the relevant information. I have learnt over the years that I have to keep an open mind on treatment. It would be very unfair of me to advocate only one form of treatment and to say that only one way works. Different approaches suit different people. I have also learnt that living one day at a time and taking responsibility for yourself is a sure-fire way to recovery. I could go on for another ten or more pages on the different types of treatment and help that are available, but really what I want to say in this chapter is that YOU ARE NOT ALONE. You are not the only person who is suffering from this condition and there is help. There are people who care and, at this very minute as you are reading this book, they are ready to help you. All you have to do is ask.

4

You're a 'human being',
not a 'human doing'

Learning to live again

Have you ever thought how preoccupied you have been, or
are with food? Let's just think about that a minute. How
much time do you actually devote to thinking about food?
Either in the eating of it, the buying of it, the preparation of
it, the smelling of it or the looking at it. I am writing this book
in between doing my sessions and in the evenings at home
and I have just had someone in my office, whose words to me
were:

> ❦ Beechy, I wake up in the morning and the very first thought
> that comes into my mind is food, and for the rest of the day
> that's it, even if I'm not eating it, I'm thinking about it. It's like
> an obsession with it, I'm looking at other people eating it, and
> thinking how lucky they are that they can have sugar or they can
> have savouries, or that they can eat like they are eating and it
> doesn't seem to have any effect on them, yet when I eat some-
> thing like that I can't stop – I just want more and more and
> more. It's like I am trying to fill this deep dark hole inside of me,
> and no matter how much I eat the feeling doesn't seem to go
> away, if anything it just seems to get bigger, am I the only person
> that feels like this, Beechy? ❧

I very quickly responded, 'No you're not. There are countless
thousands of people who are feeling like you, or have felt like
you are feeling.' Immediately she picked up on the, 'Have

felt like.' She said, 'How have they got out of it?' My answer
to her was that the people who were in recovery from their
eating disorders had decided to become 'human beings'
rather than 'human doings', and what I mean by this is that
you are not a *being, feeling* person when you are under the
merciless obsession of eating and thinking about nothing
else but food. You are controlled by the food. You are manipulated by the food. Your happiness is determined by food,
your whole day seems to be taken up obsessed with food.

Even at work, whatever occupation you have, in the office,
the factory, the shop, the supermarket, the doctor's surgery,
etc. – whatever you do – your mind will constantly be drawn
to food. So what happens is that you become someone who
is just 'doing' rather than someone who is a 'being'. Look
back at the quotation, get a picture of what is happening to
you – the preoccupation, the obsession that grinds away at
you, that takes up all your time and your energy, hampering
your creativity, your ambition and that drive you have to get
on in life. All that is happening is that you are just constantly
driven to the fridge, or to the store to buy some more food.

Some of you may be reading this chapter and thinking,
'Well I'm not that bad, that hasn't happened to me,' well put
a 'yet' on it. An eating disorder is a progressive condition. It
doesn't start off at its worse stage. Remember food has
become lots of things to you – it's a friend, it's a comfort.

An obsession out of control

Later on in the book I am going to look at how you've built
up your relationship with food, and how negative that can
become, but, for the moment, let's look at the preoccupation with food and what is happening. One person always
springs to my mind when I'm talking about this part of an
eating disorder condition, and that is a young lady that I
treated about six or seven years ago. With her permission I
have told her story many times. Sometimes the reactions I
have received have been of laughter, but the laughter has

been caused by anxiety, and the anxiety has been caused by the tragedy of this situation; of how out of control she had become with food.

She recalled to me that for as long as she could remember she had been overweight, she had always found a lot of comfort for her feelings in food and, as she became older, she became totally dependent on food. She got married and she had a daughter. Her husband, for the most part, was a very understanding man and did everything he could to try and help, but as her condition became worse he couldn't bear the situation any more and he had to leave. One afternoon in my office she recalled to me how she felt when her husband left with her daughter. She said, 'A part of me was destroyed and devastated, but another part was happy because this voice said to me in my head, "Now you can eat what you want, now you don't have to hide the food, now you don't have to eat it on the way home, now you don't have to lie about how much money you are spending on food. (If you're spending all that money on food where is the food?) Now you don't have to explain anything any more, because you can eat it, and eat as you want and not have to feel anything or explain anything to anyone ".' She talked about how all of a sudden her eating disorder really manifested itself into a total nightmare. She explained to me that she always had a favourite plate from which she would eat her food. It was her favourite plate because it was larger than any other plate in the house and because she could easily pile her food up on it. She talked about one afternoon whilst in the middle of a binge, she was eating off this plate and all of a sudden she looked over at her dustbin and she had an idea. So she got up, she took the lid off the dustbin and went out to the garden shed to where her husband kept his DIY tools, she sawed the handle off the dustbin lid and came back into the kitchen where she turned it over on its back so that it balanced and it looked like an enormous plate with a dip in it. She covered it in tin foil and started to eat out of that.

I sat opposite her and, as she was telling me this, I tried to get a picture of someone sitting in the midst of turmoil and

suddenly getting up, taking a dustbin lid, sawing the handle
off and turning it over so that she could have it as an even
bigger plate. I got this mental picture of her sitting at her
table eating out of a dustbin lid covered in tin foil. I thought,
my God, how chronic does this illness get? How much does
it take of a person's self-respect, dignity and sense of reality?
But, if that wasn't bad enough, she went on to tell me that
she stopped using the dustbin lid, and just started eating off
of the work surfaces.

Now you may be reading this and thinking, 'Oh for
heaven's sake, this is just ridiculous,' but I kid you not. There
may be some of you reading this who will know these feelings. There may be some of you who have perhaps not used
a dustbin lid as a plate, but you may have eaten out of dust-
bins; and there may be some of you reading this who have
actually ran out of food at some time in your kitchen, so have
decided to eat the cat food or dog food. I'm talking about a
condition that has no boundaries. Yes, you might not have
done these things, but it's possible because that incessant
craving for food can become totally out of control. You also
may be thinking, 'Oh he's just saying these things to be a sen-
sationalist, or to keep my attention to read this book. Believe
me, I'm not. I'm telling you the truth, and there are so many
people who can verify what I'm saying.

What I am actually trying to get across to you is the sadness
– the unhappiness, the isolation, the alienation – those feelings of no self-worth that an eating disorder can induce in a
person. Surely you will agree with what I have just told you.
It's not a story about a 'human being', but a 'human doing'.
It really is the same scenario as the alcoholic – once he has
that first drink he can't stop. Once you have that first bite
more than you should have, or once you have the first taste
of something that you really crave for, you can't stop until it's
finished. Even then, sometimes, you have to go and get more
because it never feels as though it's finished. It's like when
people used to say to me, 'Oh Beechy, just have one drink'.
When was one drink ever good enough? It's like someone
saying to you, 'Just have one cream cake – just have one

pretzel – just have one crisp – just have one . . . When was one ever good enough for you? When did one ever fill the gap? That hole? That emptiness that you eat on?

As I am writing this chapter I'm thinking, 'Oh gosh, am I saying these things too early in this book? Am I going to frighten people away from reading any further? Maybe I should keep it until later on in the book', but I can't, I've got to let you know now about how serious things can get, or maybe how serious they already are for you. But I'm also saying to you that there is a way out of this.

Taking responsibility

There is a way to deal with this preoccupation and these devastating consequences do not have to continue in your life if you are willing to do something about it: if you are willing to take responsibility, if you are actually willing to acknowledge and to admit how powerless you have become over food, how it has taken over your life, and everything else in your life. That is the first step, that is what we are really talking about, you taking the first step and actually saying to yourself, 'Yes this is me. I may not have all these consequences, but I have these feelings, and I can identify with what is being said to me and I have to do something about it.' Your husband can't do it. Your wife can't do it. Your kids can't do it. Your mother-in-law or father-in-law can't do it. Your aunts and uncles can't do it. Your employers can't do it. No one can take that first step but you. Nor should you do it for them. You have got to do it for you, because you are the one who is worth something. You are the one who can achieve something through all of this. It's got to be you.

Remember what you were like before you started using food? Can you remember when you were happy? Or when you just got on with your life and enjoyed things? Maybe you were involved with sport? Can you remember how good it was to be fit? How your body felt? Can you remember how much energy you had and how committed and competitive you were? How good did it feel to be a part of something, to be part of a team and to be doing something that you really enjoyed? How much of that have you got today? How fit are you? How much enjoyment are you having? How much are you using the potential that you have? How hard is it for you to get motivated? I'm talking about you getting back to the old you – the you that was happy, the you that had a choice. That is something that you haven't had for a long time – a choice, and especially around food. A choice just to eat something that you enjoy, and feel satisfied. A choice to look after your body. A choice for you to deal with your feelings honestly, directly and assertively, without any fear of shame, remorse or guilt or what people will think. It's about having a choice to be you, rather than living your life through, or for other people or doing everything for everybody else and nothing for you. I know you know that one!

You could also say to me, 'Beechy, I don't know who I am. I don't know how I really feel about myself, I've never thought like this before and, if I'm honest, the thought of this really frightens me.' I agree with you. It is frightening but really the fear that you are experiencing is about going into the unknown, because I am asking you to take some risks with yourself. I am asking you to start to confront what has been actually happening in your life rather than continually eating on all the feelings that you never really talk about and to ask you to come out of this 'state of denial' that there is nothing wrong. I am asking you to do something that you have really never done before, and that is to be fearlessly honest with yourself about what is happening to you because that is the way it is going to have to be if you really want to get well.

There are no half measures or short cuts. You can diet as much as you want, but the diet has to stop somewhere, and your reality has to come back, which is when the old scenario starts over again, and back you go on to that 'treadmill', onto that 'merry-go-round'. You usually only find merry-go-rounds in funfairs. Well, I don't know about you, but I haven't heard anything funny in what I've been talking about so far. When I see people who are very overweight. I see unhappiness, I see emotional pain, I see people who are trying to cope in a way that doesn't help them. When I see people who are so thin, anorexic, I see people who are doing the same thing, only it's in reverse. It's the punishment – the self loathing – trying to control something that is out of control. For people that are inducing vomiting and taking laxatives it's still the same scenario – it's still the same chaos – trying to control something that is again, out of control, but using something else to try to get rid of it.

There's a war on – and it's called the 'WEIGHT WAR' . . . and all you have to do to WIN this war is stop fighting, stop getting back in the ring only to be beaten, stop numbing your feelings and face your fears. I know that you can do this because I have treated countless people who have, and they are now 'human beings' *not* 'human doings'.

5

Start now!

Look to today, not the future

OK! We need to get going with this. What you do today is the start of changing tomorrow, but you must stop putting it off. It's no good saying that, 'Tomorrow I'm going to be different.' You see it isn't a question of being different – it is a question of allowing yourself to change some things. I always say to people, 'Keep doing what you have been doing and you will keep getting what you already have.' So if you want something to be different you need to think again about what needs to be changed in your life. You will also know by now that focusing solely on the food is another reason why things don't change for you. You see it is a question of asking yourself, 'what is really eating you' rather than, 'I've got to stop eating that and that and that, etc. . . . '

The only place you can start is here and now. You can't change the diet that went wrong two months ago or the plans that you have in six months' time.

You will remember that I talked about a food plan at the beginning of the book. I want you to go back to that now, if you haven't thought about it since you started the book. You see you must have a plan. If someone has developed a really serious drinking problem they will follow a programme of abstinence: they will stop drinking alcohol. They will, of course, continue to drink other fluids. You need to be aware of your own abstinence plan. Of course you can't stop eating, as the alcoholic can't stop drinking fluids, so you need to know where your goalposts are. Once you make the decision to set them you shouldn't keep moving them because that is when the problems start to take hold. That does not mean, however, that you can't change your plan in time.

Food plan outline

1. Eat three meals a day, do not snack in between, and ensure that these meals are taken at regular intervals.

2. If you are medically overweight then aim to eat in order to reduce your weight gradually. Do not attempt to eat minimally because this simply fuels binges, i.e. you get so hungry that you lose control.

3. For those of you struggling with anorexia the same plan applies, but ensure that you are eating sufficiently and aim to increase your weight slowly. I know that you will need help with this, but please bear with me for the time being. Please also be aware that once food is on your plate it must be eaten. (Those of you who are very underweight may need to incorporate snacks until you are ready to eat only three meals a day).

4. If you are following an exercise plan, please note that a reasonable limit is to exercise three times per week for twenty minutes. If you are really overexercising then it will be necessary to look towards reducing this.

5. Avoid sugar and 'binge' foods. Those of you who are compulsively overeating, or experience a starving-bingeing cycle will be able to identify binge-type foods and should work towards excluding them from your diet. Sugar is extremely important to avoid. For those of you suffering from anorexia, and are greatly underweight, it will be important to eat in order to reach a medically acceptable weight.

Personal plan

This plan must be in accordance with your medical
condition and I would suggest that you speak to your
general practitioner before embarking upon a diet and
exercise routine.

....

....

....

....

....

....

....

....

Please write down your own plan in the space left for you.
Use a separate piece of paper if you need more room. You
need a sense of direction, so please take time to write it. It
should include the number of meals you will have, and consider the approximate times that you will have these. You also
need to be making a commitment to how much weight you
will either lose or gain.

Please remember when you write this plan that it should be
somewhere within the realms of what I have suggested, and
that if you need to obtain medical advice, because you are
very over or underweight, you should incorporate what the
medical practitioner suggests. I am not going to encourage
you to do anything that is not good for your general health.
Here is a plan that one of my patients did for me last year:

Jane's revised plan

PRESENT WEIGHT: 16 stone

WEEKLY WEIGHT LOSS: Minimum of 2.5 lbs per week

TARGET WEIGHT: 11 stone (at the moment) – I will review it in a couple of months.

FOOD PLAN:
- Eat three meals a day.
- Abstain from sugar (especially as I binge on chocolate).
- Avoid white bread, cheese, crisps and 'snack foods'.
- I will eat three meals a day because I tend to avoid eating during the day when I am dieting and then I get so hungry I go mad.

EXERCISE PLAN:
- I am going to start walking my children to school rather than driving.
- I am going to swim twice a week.
- When I am fitter I will join an exercise class.

TRIGGER SITUATIONS:
I always tend to lose control in the following situations:
- When I am angry.
- When I feel that there is no point because I have 'gone off' my diet slightly.
- When I am feeling worthless.

I know that I can help myself in these areas by:
- Talking to someone when I feel angry. I am also going to keep a diary and use it to talk about my feelings if I can't speak to anyone.
- I am not going to move the goalposts.
- I am going to start to treat myself as if I am worth more – breaking my compulsive overeating is going to help that.
- I am going to attend meetings of Overeaters Anonymous twice a week because I can get a lot of support from them.
- I can't afford any more therapy sessions at the moment but

I am going to save the money that I would have spent on food and have five more therapy sessions.

You can see from this plan that a lot of important decisions have been made.

It is important to be realistic when compiling your plan – do not attempt too much too soon. Below is Jane's first attempt at this exercise:

Jane's first plan

PRESENT WEIGHT: 16 stone

WEEKLY WEIGHT LOSS: 8 lbs

TARGET WEIGHT: 9½ stone

FOOD PLAN:
- Eat three meals a day.
- Just one piece of fruit for breakfast and lunch and small salad (no potatoes or bread).
- If I can, I will skip a meal.

EXERCISE PLAN:
Go to an aerobics class and swim every day.

TRIGGER SITUATIONS:
Never thought about it.

HOW CAN YOU HELP YOURSELF FURTHER
I can't and no one can support me.

This plan is destined to fail and there are probably so many of you who would recognize this drastic action that simply can't be kept up. Even if you do keep it up it will be bad for your health.

Key nutritional points

1. Eat a balanced meal choosing from:
- Carbohydrates* (wholemeal bread, brown rice, pasta, potatoes, oats, unsweetened breakfast cereals).
- Vegetables, salads and fruit.
- Protein (chicken, fish, lean meat, pulses, beans and eggs).
- Dairy products (milk, yoghurt, cheese – low-fat versions if you need to lose weight).

N.B. Restrict your intake of fats, both:
Added (butter, oil, margarine), and
Hidden (salami, pastry, biscuits, etc.)

* A note regarding CARBOHYDRATES:
This food group includes
– SUGARS, e.g. chocolate, jam and honey
– STARCHES, e.g. potatoes, pasta
– HIGH-FIBRE POLYSACCHARIDES, e.g. brown rice, wholemeal bread
All three are composed of chains of simple sugar building blocks, but the length of the chains and overall structure varies.

- SUGARS
These should be avoided as they are composed of short chains of simple sugars and break down in the digestive system quickly, causing the blood sugar level to rise too rapidly. This elevation is followed by a rapid drop in blood glucose which triggers a craving for more sugary foods to be eaten.

- STARCHES and HIGH-FIBRE POLYSACCHARIDES
These should be taken in preference to sugars as they take longer to break down into their component sugar building blocks (See next diagram.)

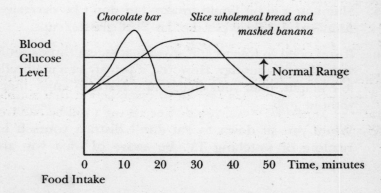

The diagram on page 53 shows that a chocolate bar gives an immediate release of blood glucose, but this only lasts for 15–20 minutes, and then the blood sugar drops and the person feels as though they require more sugary foods to feel better. However, a slice of wholemeal bread and mashed banana gives a steady, slower rise and fall of blood glucose, better stamina and no cravings for sugary foods as it is rich in long chain starches.

2. ● Avoid added hidden refined sugars.
    ● Avoid white flour products, especially if these are trigger foods for you. Eat wholegrain bread, pasta, brown rice, etc.
    ● Avoid any trigger or binge foods such as peanuts, cheese, etc.

3. If you need to lose weight you should aim to do so *slowly* and eventually combine weight loss with exercise to shift stubborn inches. Don't use scales as your parameter of success. Look in the mirror, notice how your clothes fit better and feel looser, and how you look healthier.

4. If you are at a very low weight, aim to eat regularly from a balanced selection of foods, 'little and often', especially if your appetite is poor or you suffer from stomach bloating. Start with comfortable portion sizes, gradually building them as your appetite increases, and move towards eating three meals a day.

5. Maintain a good liquid intake, but don't be excessive. Aim for 1.5–2 litres per day. i.e. 7–10 glasses/cups.

6. If you need to lose weight *avoid* snacks, eat three evenly spaced meals per day. However, if you are at a medically low weight, plan your snacks and learn to enjoy them without guilt.

7. When you sit down to eat don't distract yourself by reading or watching TV. Be aware of what you are eating.

8. Avoid alcohol as this can enhance the appetite and impair your judgement.

9. Don't expect miracles overnight. It may take time, but it will be worth it.

It is also very important not to set yourself impossible targets or deliberately set out on a course that will lead you to instant failure. This is why you must take some time to think about your plan. Remember that this plan is personal and you may not wish to discuss it with friends and family. Often it is better just to get on with something rather than to make a big announcement. This plan should be more like a way of life than anything else.

To help you a bit more I want you to do several other things for me. Firstly, I want you to think about your worst day of bingeing, starving, overeating or whatever comprises your worst time. Then I want you to be really honest with yourself and think about what, in that day, you really want to avoid. I'm sure that this will help you with your plan. You see, no matter what you may say to people on the outside, I know that what you do to yourself does not make you happy, but you can't see a way out and this is what keeps you doing these things.

For those of you who are at medical risk, e.g. very overweight, underweight, using a lot of laxatives or inducing vomiting many times a day, I would ask you to consider seeking further support if you find that you cannot stick to this plan. It may be that with a bit of extra help things will become easier for you.

Those of you suffering from anorexia will probably be saying, 'I'm alright, I don't want to put on any weight,' but I know deep down how frightened you will be and how a part of you will know that you have truly lost control, i.e. you cannot allow yourself to eat.

When you are very underweight, and have not been eating for a while, you will feel 'stoned' and this will make you feel as if there is nothing wrong with you. One of the things you have to do before you can think clearly is to start to eat sufficiently to recover from the battering you've given your body. Once you are no longer a concern medically, it is time to think for yourself. I know that you will be feeling angry at what I'm saying. I understand that when a person gets so unhealthy that they need medical intervention, it is normal for them to get angry at being controlled. But I also believe that if you truly want to be independent, you must get out of this trap of having to be controlled.

In the same way, when you are overweight, all conversations are about your weight, and whether or not you should go to your doctor because of a condition related to your weight. I am sure that you get sick of comments made in the street about your weight.

Looking after yourself

So it is time for a change and for the real you to emerge from behind the weight. From now on I hope that you can learn to be good to yourself on several different levels:

- Feeling or emotional level, i.e. allow yourself the ability to feel and express feelings. I suppose this is called 'living in reality'.
- Physical level, i.e. show care and respect for your body by eating properly and healthily; keep good personal hygiene; dress yourself to the best of your ability and be good to yourself.
- Mental level, i.e. work on your ability to learn, grow and change.
- Social level, i.e. begin or continue to develop and maintain meaningful relationships. To love and be loved are basic needs.
- Spiritual level, (not to be confused with religion!) i.e. your ability to be in touch with whatever gives your life meaning.
- Level of will, i.e. your ability to take responsibility for yourself.

Look again at these six levels. How much has your eating disorder affected these areas? Perhaps this too can be a challenge to get to work on yourself as a whole person.

Remember, once you have decided on your plan you must stick with it. Food needs to take its rightful place in your life. You need to 'eat to live', not 'live to eat'.

Food, my friend, my enemy

It is so important to understand why you 'use' food. Either starving, bingeing, purging, controlling or compulsively overeating. I don't think that it is good enough to say: 'Well I just can't help it' or 'That's me, isn't it?' Think about the harm you do to yourself when you give all your power away to food. Let's put it another way. You aren't what you eat, or how you eat, but your eating does or is saying something about you. It's time to look again at your relationship with food and say or write down what is going on.

Diary

Start to keep a diary. Don't let anyone see it but start to really look at yourself and your relationship with food. What happens in you day? How are you *really* feeling? rather than translating everything into hunger or a need to avoid food.

Keep this up for a while and *really* be honest in it. This is going to help you to see what is really happening.

Lots of people say 'I love food' and they sit in my office dangerously overweight with high blood pressure. So you love something so much that you are prepared to let it kill you? I think not.

Overeating obviously relieves, soothes, pushes down and anaesthetise, so you need to be considering the possibility of doing something else with your feelings. You don't have to risk your health in this way or believe that there are not other ways to cope.

COSTS AND BENEFITS

When you are ready, I want you to take a piece of paper and divide it into two. On one side I want you to look at the benefits of your use of food and on the other side the costs.

For example

BENEFITS	COSTS
I stop feeling angry or sad.	I sweat a lot.
	High blood pressure.
I like eating (at the time).	I feel ill.
	I feel so bad about myself.
	I can't wear the clothes I'd like to wear.
	My children are embarrassed by my weight.

These are just a few of the costs and benefits. Take your time to look at these. You will only feel the need to make changes if you weigh these up.

Please make your own list.

If you are starving you may say that food is your enemy, but I know that there will be a part of you that is *dying* to eat. You too might like to do the costs and benefits exercise. Have a look at the costs and benefits of your starving:

For example

BENEFITS	COSTS
I don't feel anything.	I am tired all the time.
I 'feel' in control.	I get sore sitting for long periods.
	I row with my family.
	I sit alone most of the time.
	I don't laugh anymore.

If you are bingeing and purging:
For example

BENEFITS	COSTS
I can eat what I want and stay slim.	I hate myself for inducing vomiting – I feel disgusting. I have ruined my teeth from the acid, and my throat is often sore. I am terrified that someone will find out. I often don't care what I look like because I get so disgusted.

If you are overexercising and controlling your food:
For example

BENEFITS	COSTS
I 'look good'. I like the discipline. I feel in control.	I don't feel good about myself no matter what I do with exercise or food. I am so preoccupied that I have little time for anything else. I am not expressing myself.

The costs can certainly be broken down into several areas:

EMOTIONAL You will often experience mood swings, tending towards feelings of depression and resulting from feelings of hopelessness and being out of control.

BEHAVIOURAL You will start to behave in a way that will be against how you 'like' to behave, e.g. experiencing anger.

SOCIAL You may withdraw from friends, or find that friends pull away from you because they are concerned about your behaviour.

LEGAL People can resort to having to steal food from

shops or steal money in order to buy food.

MARITAL   It becomes difficult to have fulfilling relationships either emotionally or physically – as a result there
will be disharmony.

PROFESSIONAL   Your problem will be affecting all areas
in your life. If you work it is likely that your ability to concentrate will be greatly affected and you are bound to take
time out from work either through absence or just 'pop-
ping out'.

INTELLECTUAL   Your ability to think is bound to be
impaired.

EDUCATIONAL   You are not going to perform as well as you
could. Preoccupation will easily damage concentration.

FINANCIAL   You are bound to spend extensive amounts of
money, particularly if you are bingeing.

HEALTH   Look back at the end of Chapter 1. The medical
consequences of bingeing, purging, starving and compulsive overeating are very high. You need to be aware of
exactly what you are doing to your body.

'Trapped in the fridge'

When I am working with clients with eating disorders I give
them lots of assignments, but without a doubt the most
revealing one is a collage entitled 'Trapped in the fridge'. I
ask my clients to put on paper, either in photographs or cuttings from magazines, their feelings of what it's like to feel
trapped with food or trapped in the fridge. The result of this
assignment never fails to show the devastating effects that an
eating disorder causes.

Compulsive overeating and binge eating are about pain
and preoccupation with food. As I said earlier in the book,
'You don't get big by looking at it.' You may have heard this
comment before, 'I just have to look at food and I put on
weight', but you know as well as I do that this is not the case.
It is time to confront this behaviour in order to release the
weight that you are carrying around with you. It is time to

have a good long look at the preoccupation you have with food, the lengths that you are willing to go to protect this preoccupation, and the lies that you are willing to tell to cover up the lies that you have already told.

Maybe some of the things that I am going to refer to in this chapter haven't happened to you yet, but if you have got this far in the book, you must be identifying with a large part of it. So what do I mean by preoccupation? How soon after you wake up do you think about eating? Or not eating? What percentage of your day is taken up by thinking about food? Or how many guilty feelings do you have about the latest broken diet? (The one that you promised you weren't going to fail at – the one that you resolutely told yourself was going to work.) Does it seem that there is no time in the day left to think about anything other than food? Or the next diet? Or some other plan that you are trying to concoct to help yourself lose weight?

Have you noticed that there just doesn't seem to be any time left in the day? Is it any wonder, therefore, that it seems so difficult to break away from the preoccupation with food. You see when something has been taking up so much time, it is no wonder that it seems too enormous to be able to make any changes. Or let me say it another way, how many times have you said, when it comes to changing your habits, that it all seems so much like hard work. But if you put the same amount of effort that the preoccupation with your problem has taken up, into other things, you will find that you will have results beyond your belief. You see it doesn't seem too much to expect when you say let's just put all the energy that I used bingeing and starving into doing something very different. This is about getting out of that trap.

The first thing to do is to *start to get honest* about the preoccupation you have been having. Ask yourself the question, 'How much have you been living a lie?' What do I mean? Well, I mean just that – how much have you been living a lie about your food? For example, have you ever been standing at the queue in the checkout and then, all of a sudden, it's your turn and you've got so many sweets or savouries, or there is more food than you would normally have; you start to feel embarrassed and you start to wonder what the check-out lady is thinking. You make some comment like, 'Oh God, another children's party!' or 'Oh heavens, it's another dinner party again' or 'Gosh, isn't it amazing how much kids eat, they never seem to get full up!'

This isn't me making up this scenario, I have heard this from numerous people who have been in this position, where they have just bought so much food and they feel so embarrassed and self-conscious, and feel that everybody is looking at how much food they've bought; but maybe people aren't looking. However, that is not the point. It's that inner feeling of guilt and the fear that someone is going to notice, or maybe bumping into someone you know and they'll make a comment about the amount of food in your basket. Maybe that's not the only supermarket you've been in that day, maybe it's your second or third because you're trying to avoid the embarrassment, so you bought a certain amount of food in each. Is this a normal way to behave? Is this the way everybody goes about their shopping? I doubt it very much.

Even as I am writing this, I am thinking, God what must this feel like to be trapped like this? To have to start to tell lies about how much food you are buying because you don't want anyone to know how much you're eating. But you know, you know how much you're eating, and you know that this isn't right. You know there is something wrong; and day by day by day it gets worse and the preoccupation gets bigger, just as the alcoholic hides alcohol, people with eating disorders hide food. The loneliness in all of this is terrible, because who can you tell? Who can you actually go to and say, 'I'm out of control with my food, I'm hiding it around the house so that my husband or my wife or my kids can't find it' or 'I'm bingeing in the bathroom' or 'I'm bingeing in the spare room' or 'I hide a lot of chocolates and sweets in the garage, garden shed or under the beds.'

Who can you tell?

And what would they think of you? It's the shame involved in all of this, the shame of being out of control with something that is supposed to be pleasurable – something that is only supposed to keep you alive. But for you it has become a merciless obsession and one that only seems to be getting worse because, however much you try to control it, it seems to be getting more and more out of control and you become more and more trapped, and your feelings of rejection become enormous.

How are your family feeling?

Have you ever stopped to consider your family for a moment? Have you wondered what your children are thinking? Or what your husband is thinking? Or your girlfriends? Or if you are a man with an eating disorder what your wife is thinking? Or your colleagues at work? They know that something is wrong, they'll be able to tell by your behaviour. They may not be able to pinpoint what you are doing but they'll know that something is not right. If you do have children you'll know that children need energy around them; where has all your energy gone? You never feel like playing any sports with your children, you don't feel like going out for walks, you don't feel like taking part in any school activities with them, or parents' days or sports days. Try to get the picture. You are not the only one who is suffering.

For every person with an eating disorder there are at least five people around them who will also be suffering, and more often than not, it is the family. The family have to tolerate the mood swings, the outbursts of anger, the long periods of silence, etc. A little bit further on in the book I'm going to think more about the family, but now is as good a time as ever to start to think about them. Although you are suffering major consequences from your eating disorder, it is working its way out to other people. So there is even more reason to get out of this trap and more reason to say, 'I am going to do something about myself – I am going to make a decision – I am going to change this.'

Assignments

I would like to give you an assignment. In fact, I would like to give you *two* assignments. The first one is to write down on a piece of paper as many examples as you can of your preoccupation with food. Be specific, and be very honest because it is important that you get a picture of just how preoccupied you are with food, and remember this assignment is for you. I am not asking you to show it to anyone else, this is private – it is personal. It is to help you get a picture of what is happening and, hopefully, to drive you to start making some decisions as to what you might change.

The second assignment is the one I talked about at the very start of this chapter. How would you like to do the collage of being trapped in the fridge with all your feelings? Get a large piece of white paper and picture yourself trapped within the corners of the paper. Look through some old magazines or, if you are good at drawing, maybe you could sketch how you are trapped in the fridge, but if not, you can use old pictures or old cuttings to depict how your feelings are not being expressed properly, and how you are using the food to numb all those feelings. If this sounds silly and too much like hard work, please please do it anyway because you will quickly see what is happening to you and it will give you a very clear picture of what you need to do to break out of this trap and head towards your freedom from the obsession of food.

As I said about the other assignment, you don't have to show it to anybody, this is for you. YOU are going to get well for YOU, you are not getting well for other people. Other people are going to get the benefits when you get well, but at the moment it has got to start from you.

You have got to make the first step and these two assignments are going to help you do that. They are going to help you get a picture of how food is ruling your life, and how it is getting in the way of you having any sense of normality. So let's start! Make a list of how preoccupied you are with your food, and then let's make a start on the collage. Don't try and rush the collage, take your time with it, you can take a few days, you can take a week, you can take a fortnight – as long as you want. The more thought you put into it and the more honest you are with this assignment, the more you will get out of it. Remember, you are worth doing this for. You are worth fighting for as much as anybody else, you deserve a chance to break free from this obsession and have some happiness in your life.

6
You are worth more than this

Don't let anxieties pull you down

We have spoken a lot about feelings in this book and, of course, the need to identify potential danger times for you such as feeling:

Angry
Sad
Lonely
'Tired' – which can often be anger in disguise
'Hungry' – which can often be so many feelings in disguise.

It is also important to be able to identify whether these feelings are really about you or concerning other people. Let me put it another way. How many times do you look at other people and feel angry with them when you are really angry with yourself, and how many times are you genuinely angry with other people and turn that anger on yourself. Do you hear what I am saying? So often whatever is going on with you is ultimately turned upon yourself rather than speaking to someone about it or facing your anger and not having to punish yourself with it.

So often compulsive overeating, bulimia and anorexia are experiences that are related to situations and feelings that have not been dealt with in the past. These problems can also be acts of anger towards yourself. So whichever way you turn

with your eating disorder it will always ultimately be you who
suffers. Say, for example, there has been some 'triggering
event' that led you into discovering your potential for
anorexia. (As I said, I believe that some people do have a pre-
disposition to this problem and it is not about weakness or
scheming.) This triggering event could be, for example, that
you have failed your exams at eighteen and your parents are,
what you perceive as, pressurising you to go back to school.
You will react to this situation because you too are feeling
upset, and you're afraid that your parents feel ashamed at
your lack of success. So you think that they are ashamed of
you and that you are no good. Team that with how you are
feeling – yes, you are disappointed and you feel angry with
yourself – and your self-confidence and self-esteem will be at
an all time low. How likely are you able to be really honest
when you are feeling like this? You can't sit down and say,
'Mum, Dad I feel awful, I feel that I have let you down, and
what is more I feel a real failure.' So this activity called
anorexia takes over. What better way to state how bad you
feel? And as long as it goes unaddressed, especially that self-
loathing, how can you stop? How can you stop that starving
and say to yourself, 'I am worth more than this?'

The way through and out for all these problems lies in
several very distinct areas:

Talking it through

If someone is worrying you or has worried you, you need to
be able to talk about things or at least write things down if
you really find it difficult to talk. If you need to talk to someone about how you feel because your upset is to do with
them, this could be sufficient. What none of us can expect
is for another person to immediately accept our point of
view or say that they are 100 per cent to blame for the
problem.

There has been a lot in the media recently about families
being split up as a result of therapists encouraging clients to

blame and be angry with parents. Yes, sometimes parents don't do a perfect job, but how do parents learn to be good parents, and how do they know what is best? Sometimes they genuinely don't know what to do and that is why talking over problems is so important – although not in an accusing or judgemental way. I have seen so many relationships heal through talking and both sides making a concerted effort to understand the other.

Sometimes parents have their own problems through ill health, psychiatric problems, alcoholism, etc., and they can't always function as they should. So if you feel that there are things you need to talk about – go for it! If you don't want to tackle it alone you can always get help from a counsellor or a therapist. You may find that even if there is no resolution you can at least know that you have said what has been bothering you. Remember also that acceptance is nothing to do with saying 'it didn't matter' or 'it didn't hurt'.

Many years ago I worked with a young man who started compulsively overeating around the time that he discovered he had been adopted. He believed that because he was not the 'real child' of his adopted parents, he was second best and he could not get this out of his head. He turned to food originally as a source of comfort and gained more and more weight. He then turned his nightmare into reality. His parents tried to encourage him to diet and he read this as confirmation that his parents were ashamed of him, and this just fueled his self-doubt and loathing. What was more, he would occasionally look in the mirror and experience such self-disgust. Sadly, the only way he knew how to deal with this was to eat more and more until he realized that there had to be another way.

The first thing he needed to do was to reduce his weight and to start talking to his parents. He first had some counselling sessions and discovered that some of the fears that he had about being second best had been founded upon snippets of information gained by listening at doors and telephone conversations. He discovered that he had really misunderstood some things and, more importantly, he had never felt that he could talk to his adoptive parents about his adoption because he felt that it would upset them. He realized that he had allowed self-doubt to grow until it had nearly overtaken him via his compulsive overeating.

Facing reality

Treating yourself as being 'worth more than this' is certainly to do with accepting reality and learning to cope with it. Starving, bingeing and purging can so often be the greatest escapes, except that when you run all your problems just stay where they are, waiting for you to come back. I once did a poll of how long that 'good feeling' lasted when people had been bingeing. Most people said that everything felt good until the last mouthful and then the terrible feelings were there just waiting. For those of you who purge, it also signalled that it was time to 'get rid' which for so many of you is so degrading and shameful.

I don't want to make any of this sound easy, nor am I giving you a 'quick fix'. What I want you to take from this is that there is a way out, and this way out takes hard work, involves being honest and getting in touch with reality. This is why all this abuse around food has to stop before you can really move on. It would be like me expecting an active alcoholic to be able to 'cope' with life when they haven't stopped drinking. It is impossible. Whilst you are 'using' you will be impaired and you will not be able to function as well as you think. The way out is always to remember that you are 'worth more than this' and that change is possible – I know it is, and deep down inside there is a tiny part of you that believes that too.

Being assertive

What I have really talked about so far is about being 'assertive', not angry or aggressive, but honest and open about your needs, whilst also understanding that the world will not stop revolving just because you may need something! I don't say that lightly. So many people wonder why they don't build good relationships when they are being down-right aggressive and rude, and use therapy as some excuse for this behaviour. It is one thing to be able to stop someone and say,

> ❛ Sarah, I have been avoiding you recently because I have been really annoyed with you as I feel that you let me down at the last minute. I would like to talk about it with you now as you are a good friend and I don't want it to get in the way of our relation-ship. ❜

NOT:

> ❛ Sarah, I am really angry with you about the last time we were supposed to meet up. Yet again, you selfishly cancelled at the last minute, and I am sick of your lack of consideration. ❜

Which would you respond most favourably to? Which way would evoke discussion and perhaps elicit information that may account for the last minute cancellation?

Ultimately the best method of dealing with how you are feeling would be to discuss it at the time and perhaps say, 'I feel . . . ', and ask why the meeting is being cancelled at the last moment. Again, assertive behaviour is about acting as if you are 'worth more than this'. Also, what about yourself? Yes, you seek solace in food, starving, bingeing etc., and it is you who gets hurt again.

There are many books around about assertiveness and numerous courses, so I would strongly recommend that you do some further work in this area. It is something that can help you so much. You see, your needs and your feelings count. I am not telling you that you are always right – that actually does not matter. If you feel upset about something you may need to talk about it in a non-accusing way. We are always so concerned with how people view us and we do not want to upset or offend them, but this makes us forget about ourselves. Remember that you do count. Your feelings count and ultimately if we run around boiling with anger, but not allowing ourselves to show it, we suffer. If you want to have more people in you life or want to improve existing relationships, you need to look at you and your own behaviour, and be honest about what needs to change.

Changing habits

We are also such creatures of habit . When each one of you stops to think about the amount of energy it will take to make the changes we have talked about it is important to acknowledge that it is difficult, but not impossible. Again that is also why 'going on a diet' is bad news if you have an eating disorder. You need to change your habits, not change them temporarily and then wonder why everything just goes straight back to the same way as before. Treating yourself as a worthwhile and valuable person is to say to yourself that 'my way does not work' and neither does doing diet after diet, so I really have to make some changes which are going to be permanent. This is also why things take time before they will really feel comfortable. Ask anyone who has given up smoking – they feel as though they have forgotten to do something for weeks afterwards. Well, changing your eating habits and learning to talk about problems are exactly the same. If you give yourself enough time it will become part of your routine – but if you try it for a week and give up then you are not giving yourself a chance.

I would like you to sit down when you have some time to yourself (I don't want you to be disturbed) and I would like you to think about what it would be like for you to stop doing all the things that you have been doing that have led you to pick up this book, and just imagine how things could be if you started to treat yourself better. The world may not change but I wonder what it would be like for you to feel at peace with yourself, to feel that you have had a productive

day and that you haven't abused yourself with food by bingeing, starving, overeating or overexercising. Take some time
to think. Perhaps think of someone whom you admire, and
understand that perhaps they have had to work at their confidence and building social and work skills. Imagine what
you could do with all that unused potential?

Remember, whatever you do, that you are worth more
than this. More than what you have been doing to yourself.
If there is something troubling you from the past then you
need to be able to talk about it with a trustworthy person. If
something is haunting you, don't let what happened yesterday make you pay penalties today. You *do* deserve more.

False evidence appearing real

Fear is such a driving force for people with eating disorders.
Have you noticed how fear seems to rule your life? How every
time you want to do something for yourself you always feel
frightened that you're never going to succeed; that you're
never going to finish it; and even if you do start something,
by the time you're halfway through it, you are already sabo-
taging it by telling yourself that people won't like what you
are doing; or that someone is going to ridicule it and make
you feel bad. That same old fear continually comes up and
tells you that you are no good and that you are not worthwhile and, eventually, you give in to that overriding feeling of
fear and end up doing nothing.

It's the same when you are trying to choose something to
wear before going out at night. How many times have you
stood in front of the mirror and tried practically all of your
wardrobe on before painfully deciding what to wear?
Probably everything that you tried on looked fine, but oh no,
it's that fear again and it comes up and it tells you, 'You look
silly in this, what are people going to think of you? Somebody
is bound to make some comment, someone's going to say
how fat you look, or how overweight you look, or that your
dress is too tight or your bottom looks too big, or your bust is

sticking out, or the colour doesn't suit you.' You've already decided that these comments are going to be said to you. Sometimes that feeling of fear is so overwhelming that you decide not to go out after all. So you tell your husband or your wife that you just haven't got anything to wear – that nothing fits – that you don't look good. Or maybe you'll make up some other excuse, that you've got a headache, or all of a sudden you're feeling sick, and you'll tell them to go on and have a good time. However much they tell you how nice you look, how much the colour suits you, or whatever you're wearing looks good on you, you won't believe them, because inside you've got this fear of what everybody else is going to think and as far as you're concerned, you're right.

I am not even going to ask you how you cope with the feelings, I already know, and so do you, you go for the food. You go for the very thing that causes all the fear in the first place. It would make sense if food were a remedy for fear, but it isn't. Let's look at that fear you seem to keep experiencing.

For me, fear stands for – *False Evidence Appearing Real.* 'What does he mean?' you might ask. Well, let me give you a scenario. Have you ever been asked to do something, maybe for the first time. Maybe it's something to do with standing up in front of people and making a short speech, or presenting a workshop, or taking part in an amateur dramatic play. Or maybe you've been asked to organize a function of some description. You've been really nervous, and you've been worrying yourself silly about it. You've even been dreaming about it, and you've started to go through all the scenarios of how bad it's going to be and how miserable you're going to feel, and how everybody is going to walk out. Or maybe they'll start booing at you, and you start to believe how they're going to react in the worst possible way. Then comes the night before, and you can't sleep. The big day arrives, you feel really panicky and nervous . . . but you get through it, and you do really well and none of the things you feared happened. So then all of a sudden you start to think, 'What was I worried about anyway, what was all that fear about, where did I collect all that false evidence from?' It always appears so real because we create the fear, and then we give ourselves the messages that we're going to fail, and there is no way that we're going to get it right. Breaking this pattern of behaviour is difficult, but it's something that you are going to have to do as it is holding you back.

The fear is holding you back from doing anything in your life. Think back on all the things that you haven't done, because you've always had that inner voice telling you, 'You can't do that, you'll never do it' – 'You're not good enough to do that' – 'Don't be silly, you'll never achieve that, people will laugh at you, people will be looking at you' – 'What makes you think that you can ever succeed?' It's that voice inside you that keeps telling you this stuff, and you keep listening to it.

Then, when you feel so bad about yourself, you go for the food. On and on and on this cycle goes. Well it's time for this to stop, it's time for you to break this pattern of behaviour. You have got to stop creating all this false evidence. What have you got to lose? Look what's happening in your life already. Is this good enough for you? Is this the way it was meant to be? Tell me where it is written that these things have got to happen to you, and that you have got to suffer? What is it that you've done? Now I'm sure that you can give me many of reasons why all this happens. I'm sure that you've got loads of excuses why you can't do anything, or why you can't make any progress; but I'm not going to accept them; because deep down you don't really accept them. You know that you're getting in the way of you making progress, so let's get out of the way. Let's make a start – and the first thing that you've got to do is stop listening to that voice in your head that tells you constantly that you're not worth getting well for, that you'll never complete anything that you do.

Probably, as you're reading this book, you're hearing the voice in your head, 'Well, don't listen to this rubbish! What's he talking about? This is a load of nonsense, what does he know about eating disorders? He's an alcoholic. How can he tell you to get better from an eating disorder?' That voice in your head will do anything to stop you getting well. That voice is the one, after you've declared that you'll never binge again, that will tell you you'll never eat so much, or that you'll stop throwing up, or that you'll never starve yourself again, or that you'll never take any more laxatives, and that you're really going to stop abusing your body. Her or his voice always creeps back in and says, 'Go on, stop being so silly. One little extra bite won't matter' – 'One little extra chocolate, or cookie won't hurt' – 'Just have a little second helping, it won't make any difference' – 'You've been a good girl' – 'You've been a good boy' – 'You've been on your diet' – 'Why shouldn't you after all you've been through today' – 'People don't understand you'. S/he will give you all these messages. S/he will never let up. S/he is not going to go away; and even when you get into recovery and you stop overeating, undereating or throwing up, or whatever it is that you are doing. S/he will still be there. That voice will always be there waiting on you to make a mistake.Waiting on a vulnerable moment. Really, what I'm saying is that your addiction doesn't go away. Just because you stop overeating, or whatever it is that you're doing, doesn't mean to say that you will never do these things again. I read a newspaper article recently about people who had become 'Slimmer of the Year' and had won awards from slimming clubs because they had lost 'X' amount of weight in a short space of time. A survey had been done on these people over a period of about three or four years, and the conclusions were that, although they lost an enormous amount of weight, the majority of them put the weight back on again. This is what I'm talking about. Just because you take it off doesn't give you licence to start overeating again.

I'm not talking about another diet. I'm talking about you taking it a day at a time with no days off. I'm talking about you managing your food instead of being managed by it. I'm talking about you ignoring that voice in you head that tells you that you can never do this, or that you can never achieve anything. I'm really asking you to stop listening to all that False Evidence Appearing Real. It's time to face all that fear that's been holding you back from getting well.

Now I know that I'm asking a lot from you; but I can't enable you to go on like this. I can't suggest that you go on overeating, undereating, taking laxatives or purging. How can I do that? I'm asking you to take the positive, healthy way out of this. By looking at that fear that eats away at you and facing it, and overcoming it; coming out the other side a better person, and having all the happiness that you richly deserve in your life. Maybe then, once and for all, you'll be able to look in the mirror and say, 'I'm OK – I'm worthwhile – I'm worth getting better for.'

Affirmations

There is no doubt that our society looks us up and down and judges us. You know, if you are overweight, the comments people make. You may also know what it is like to hear the words, 'What's your problem, you're slim and good looking? You surely can't have any problems!'

Some of you will also have experienced reaching your ideal weight but being devastated because, yes! you look different, but don't *feel* any different!

Working on yourself, as I have said to you all through this book, is about working on the 'inside' as well as working on your physical appearance. A further way to do this is to work on affirming yourself.

I see your recovery from food problems as repairing your relationships, stopping food controlling you and becoming physically and mentally stronger. The basis for all of this is for you to begin to repair the relationship you have with yourself. This means that you must work hard at accepting yourself. Think of all the effort you have put into eating, not eating, exercising, lying, and cheating to yourself. Well, grab all that energy and use it for yourself in a very different way.

I know that your 'eating' will have been caused by mood swings – from feeling really preoccupied and agitated about getting a binge together – to the feelings of guilt and self-loathing if you have binged or purged. The first step is to get your abstinence. Think how good you'll feel about yourself if you do stop all of that.

Take a minute to imagine not having to binge, starve, purge or compulsively exercise. Talk about what it would be like really to regain your self-respect and stop dwelling on your faults.

I have affirmed you throughout this book for staying with me and for reading and understanding what I have been saying to you. I know that some of it won't have been easy for you, as you have had to get really honest with yourself.

Do you remember me asking you, at the beginning of the book, to take a photograph of yourself and write a description of what you saw and how you felt. Well, I'd like you to do it again, repeat the exercise; and no matter how hard it is, I'd like you to note the positive changes (however small).

At this stage I am more interested in how you are feeling than what you look like. Have you praised yourself for being honest, and for being strong enough really to face up to your problem? Are you, bit by bit, learning to like yourself, or certain aspects of yourself?

I'd like you to write a list of what you like about yourself as an individual. Are you kind, generous, a good listener, a faithful friend, a good companion to your partner, etc. Please put some time into this. You need to learn to focus positively on yourself. You need to take care of yourself in all senses. Your appearance, health and mental well-being. It's one thing to take pride in your appearance and another to be obsessed. Some of you will have stopped keeping yourself clean and tidy. Make a point of changing this from today, and if you have damaged your teeth from sugar or vomiting get to the dentist. You don't have anything to be ashamed of – you are on the path to change.

How healthy and physically active are you? By that I don't mean being obsessed with exercise as some of you may be. I mean, for example, some gentle walks, or a swim. Some of you may be very over or underweight, in such cases you need to consult your doctor before exercising, and once he has given you the go ahead, be gentle and take things slowly.

Your food plan should also be part of treating yourself better. You should no longer be beating yourself up with food, purging, starving or taking laxatives.

If you have been taking yourself for granted, stop it now. Write a list of what you do in one day. Write another list of things you need to do and keep crossing things off as you complete each goal or task. Remember to affirm yourself for trying, even if you don't succeed 100 per cent.

Having an eating problem does not make you a bad or weak-willed person – remember that – and also don't forget the depths of despair your problem has dragged you down to.

Also take time to think about the things that you have done in your life. It may be that your problem has taken up a lot of your time, but remember that you can get back on top.

How you approach life is so important – you are not a loser. There is a part of you that is so strong and so capable, so start behaving as if you are strong. Start behaving as if you are capable. If it feels strange at first then you will just have to fake it. This is a time to think of goals for yourself that are outside of issues around food and weight. With each goal it is important to be realistic and set reasonable targets. Having said that, however, don't be afraid of success and understand that it is normal to feel anxious about expectations from others. I want you to watch out for old habits. Remember how easy it is for you to sabotage yourself and shut yourself in the dark.

Of course, changing for the better means living up to people's high expectations of you, but don't let that fear grip you. You have a right to act as a winner. So don't get caught in that old familiar trap of self-defeat. What is so wrong with failing sometimes?

Examining where things went wrong can be very valuable. This also applies if you should break your food plan. Stop and have a look at what has happened and at what you need to do differently to enable you to stay permanently on the plan.

You need to get into the habit of affirming yourself on a daily basis. Understand that this is an important part of your recovery from your food problems. At the end of each day, take some time to yourself – take stock of your day – and remember you are worth it.

It is so important to confront and counteract the negative messages that you are giving yourself:

I can't.
It's useless, I'm just one of those people who can't do it.
I'm fat.
I'm ugly.
If I eat properly I will be enormous, and then everyone will hate me.
I'm not worth it.

Keep telling yourself these things and you will continue believing them. You need to change these messages (just like on a music cassette – if you didn't like the sound, you'd put on another tape).

Think positively and you will eventually *act* positively, e.g:

I can do this and I am worth it.
I can do it and I am going to. It may take time but it will be OK.
Today I am overweight but I can change that.
I *feel* ugly but deep down inside I know that I am not.
I can eat properly and I will not get fat.
I AM WORTH IT.

Here are some examples of affirmations to give yourself:

I am a worthwhile person and I am going to treat myself properly.
I have done well today. I have stuck to my plan. Well done me!
Today I am going to think of five things that I like about myself and keep repeating them. (If I get stuck I will ask others to help me).

I am not a weak-willed person and I can make changes on a daily basis.

Please think of your own affirmations to add to this list.

7

You can change the habits of a lifetime

Own up to the bad ones and learn how to stop them

Before I even start to say anything in this chapter I have to ask you a question. The question is this: is what you've got, what you want? If it is, fine, keep doing what you've been doing, and you'll keep getting what you've got; but if you're not happy with what you've got, you and I have to start looking at how you can change your habits.

I'm not only talking about changing your habits with food,but changing your habits with your behaviour. There is an expression I use repeatedly in my work which is, 'Keep doing what you're doing and you'll keep getting what you've got.' Many people that I've treated with eating disorders have been trying to control their food intake, and they have been failing miserably and continually suffering the emotional pain that compulsive overeating, undereating or inducing vomiting brings.

When I use this expression with people, they get very niggled with me because the majority don't want to admit that they can't control their eating. Everybody wants to hold on to the belief that they are in charge. If you are willing to be honest with yourself, you will readily admit that you are anything but in charge of your eating. You've still got this pride inside you, that will be telling you that you still can do something about your eating in your own way. Well, if you want to get really honest, if your way is working why are you reading this book?

I also personally know what it's like to have this expression said to me. When I was drinking, someone said to me, 'Keep doing what you're doing, and you'll keep getting what you've got, Beechy,' and I couldn't stand it. I knew that they were right on one level, but all the pride inside of me was screaming, 'No, no, I'll be OK, I can do what I want, I can control my drinking,' when really everything was out of control.

It is the same with food, there is no difference. I was drinking to try to change the way I was feeling, to deal with the feelings of low self-worth and disgust about myself.

It's these same feelings that you are trying to control, only you are using food; but at the end of the day it doesn't work. I know how difficult it is to make sense of this behaviour when you are in the middle of it, but believe me you've got to start. One of the most effective ways I know of helping you to start is to ask you to draw up a self-assessment of what is going on in your life. If food is a predominating factor, let's have a look at that.

When I'm working with patients on a one-to-one basis I give them a self-assessment assignment which helps them look at the powerlessness and unmanageability of their illness. Filling in this self-assessment is the first stage of really acknowledging the power of the compulsion and the level of unmanageability caused by food. So in this chapter I am going to give you the responsibility of filling in a self-assessment as an assignment to help you recognize what is happening in your life with your eating disorder.

Exactly how you are going to benefit from this self-assessment will very much depend on how honest you are going to be with yourself because, as I've explained to you before, this is for you – the assignment isn't for anyone else. It isn't for your wife or your husband or your children. It is for you, it's about your behaviour with food, so it goes without saying that it is very important that you take this seriously. It is even more important that you are as honest as you can be with yourself. As you and I haven't met, I'm not sure what stage you have reached with your eating disorder, so I've had to set out this self-assessment rather differently than I normally would with patients with whom I am working on a one-to-one basis.

Let's have a look at the four main stages of an eating disorder:

- The early stage
- The middle stage
- The crucial stage
- The chronic stage

All of these stages have the same importance because they are interlinked. If you are thinking that just because you're at a pre-problem stage you won't move into phase two, phase three or phase four, be warned, they are most definitely interlinked.

Eating disorders follow a progressive pattern, and it is important that you and I separate what might be called normal eating from problem eating. The distinction is quite simple and clear. People who eat three meals a day and don't obsess about food (and what I mean by obsessing with food is thinking about it continually, thinking about what you're going to eat, how much you're going to eat or how little you're going to eat; or how many calories are in every meal) they enjoy the use of food. They don't overdo it. It isn't taking over their lives, and it won't be the end of the world if they eat a little bit too much, or a little bit less than they normally would. This is totally the opposite situation for someone with an eating disorder.

Early stage

People with eating disorders have immense difficulty with food, both while they're eating it and when they're not eating it. The pre-problem stage can be classified as the learning stage. You are learning that food is an enjoyable substance to have and it's nice to look at. Someone once said to me that 'People eat with their eyes', and I really believe that to be true. If you're in a restaurant and something is presented to you very nicely it will be much more enticing than something that's just been thrown on the plate where it's obvious that there has been no care taken in the preparation.

So you are learning about food, you're learning that on different social occasions it is an expected thing that certain types of meal will be eaten. Like a christening, a garden party, a barbecue, a wedding, or a formal reception. Thanksgiving, if you're an American, will involve a sit-down meal with your family, it will be a big occasion, you will be expected to have a 'Thanksgiving dinner'. At Christmas many of us will have the traditional turkey dinner. You are learning all along that food is a very sociable substance. It's a way of meeting people, and pleasing people; but if misused you will also learn that it causes chaos, torment, loneliness, anger and remorse.

Middle stage

What has happened to you is that somewhere along the way you have crossed the fine line where your eating really isn't social any more. Food has taken on a greater importance in your daily lives, and other people such as husbands, wives, children, friends, family and employees start to take second place to food. As does your work. There will be very noticeable changes in you behaviour and the way you treat people in situations that get in the way of your eating. You'll start to have angry outbursts if you're asked questions about the time taken up with eating food, and this is where that fine line is really crossed into the onset of an eating disorder.

It will be obvious that there is a definite dependence on food. You'll take risks with your eating. Everybody seems to think that it's only dangerous to drive a car while you're under the influence of alcohol, but you imagine driving down the road with one hand on the steering wheel and one hand in a packet of biscuits, or trying to open a packet of crisps or a bar of chocolate. Many accidents have been caused by drivers who have been in the middle of a binge in their car. There is also danger at work. You may have eaten far too much sugar and you may start to feel very drowsy, you could fall asleep over a machine, or start to become very forgetful because you are so preoccupied with food, and when you are next able to eat. You'll start to have feelings of isolation, remorse and guilt about your eating, but you'll be unable to express those feelings. Instead you'll start to lie about your use of food.

Crucial stage

You may even start to plan your eating binges, well ahead of time. This takes us into the crucial stage. Now you are finding it very difficult to control the amount of food that you're consuming. You'll say things like, 'Well I'm only going to have a small lunch today, or a small salad for dinner;' but it ends up in a full-scale binge. Promises are always broken. The old excuses become more and more repetitive. You start to get angry with yourself, and you start to have tantrums, and totally unrealistic resentments. You'll start to neglect yourself. Your hygiene won't be as good as it was. Less and less effort is going to be made with your personal appearance. The time between meals may be coming closer together, and it ends up that you're grazing all day. Your mood swings will become more and more unpredictable and people around you will not know how to cope with you.

Chronic stage

Can you get the picture of what is happening to you? Can you see what you're becoming? Because now you're entering into the chronic stage. You become totally obsessed with food. More and more you lose touch with what is happening in your day and you become more and more isolated from your feelings. While all this is happening to you, you'll obviously not be looking after your family, whether you're a wife or a husband. You won't be looking at anyone else's needs, how can you when all this is happening to you? You may be losing more and more time from work or your time keeping may start to suffer. Your work performance is going to become very poor, and your relationships with colleagues or clients are going to be disturbed. Your concentration will suffer because you'll be concentrating more on food. Your critical faculties and thought processes will become progressively duller. You may also be coming into financial difficulties because of your eating.

This progressive disregard for yourself and others will result in gradual disregard for everything else around you. You'll deteriorate spiritually, and you'll lose trust and faith in yourself and others. Further deterioration will continue in all physical aspects of your health and fitness. Life becomes a total preoccupation with food.

I am not saying that all these things are happening to you right now, but I will guarantee that they will happen if you have entered into any of these four stages. They are so interlinked that they have to follow each other. An eating disorder is a progressive illness. It will not suddenly stop and stay the same – it gets progressively worse. The above four stages have been researched and written about more extensively by people in the field of alcoholism. I have taken these same four stages and transposed them to help people with eating disorders. I personally see dependence on alcohol as no different from dependence on food.

I have sat in countless groups, and listened to people share consequences of their drinking, eating or drug addiction, and the feelings are the same. I see the whole gamut of chemical dependencies as feelings, and people use the substances to medicate those feelings. As I said in the book I wrote on alcohol, dependence on alcohol is a progressive pattern – I see the same in eating disorders.

However, the progress is not always in a straight line. Some

people with eating disorders can become deluded into thinking that they are OK and everything is fine, because they
don't binge all the time, or because they can continually go
on diets and lose some weight, but look at what happens to
them when they come off the diet – they put the weight back
on. Other people delude themselves into saying things like,
'Oh well, I'm OK now, everything is fine, I've stopped eating
sugar, I've stopped eating too much pasta and I'm not eating
nearly as much bread as I used to.' But what happens is that
the food creeps back in, and everything isn't alright, and
they go right back to square one. Once the dependency on
food has got to this level there really is no controlling it
UNLESS YOU SEEK SOME HELP, or some intervention is
made with you. I cannot emphasize enough the importance
of doing a self-assessment.

Self-assessment

Once again, I have to say to you that if you're not going to be
rigorously honest about yourself, you won't get the full benefit of what this can bring. It is so important to take a look at
what you've been doing with food, and the way you've been
behaving around food. This assessment will help you to get
the full picture of how powerless you really are when it comes
to food. If you're really willing to be honest and take a good
look at yourself, this will be the most important step that you
will ever take in helping yourself with your eating disorder.

The self-assessment should take you about a week, if done
properly. You may say that this seems like an awfully long
time, but think about it, you need to sit down and ask yourself some serious questions, and I'm going to ask you to think
long and hard about those questions. I want you to write
down on separate pieces of paper specific examples on each
topic, and when you've finished this you'll have a very clear
picture of what's been happening to you in all aspects of your
life regarding your eating disorder.

To get the most out of this self-assessment you need to be

specific in all your answers to the questions, and give at least two or three examples for each answer, e.g. where and when the situation happened, was there anybody else involved? What was your behaviour like at that time? How much were you eating at the time? Take plenty of time with each example because this is very important. Think back, try to remember as much as you can about the situation and who else was involved? Or maybe you were on your own? Be as thorough as you can. Don't forget, this is a very important part of you looking at your eating disorder, it's the most important step that you're going to take. Try not to exaggerate, minimize or trivialize any of the situations that you're going to write about. Try to answer the questions in numerical order, and don't forget, take your time, don't rush. Get everything down on paper. The more you put down, the more you'll see what is happening to you, and just how much food is affecting your life.

I can't stress this enough. If you decide to stop doing what you're doing, you really will stop getting what you've got. You will move into a phase of happiness and control in your life that you could never imagine.

So it's time to start, it's time to take this first step, so get some paper, a pen and a quiet place and let's start with the self-assessment:

In this assessment I want you to be really honest with yourself. Remember this is for you, you don't have to show this to anyone.

Self-assessment assignment

Please answer the following with specific examples. Each example should state:

(a) Where and when the situation happened?
(b) Who else was involved?
(c) What your behaviour was like?
(d) What you were eating at the time (really think about the quantities)? Give at least two or three specific examples.

Section I – Compulsiveness

This section will help you explore just who is in control. Do you really believe it is you?

In what ways has your overeating, starving or inducing vomiting led to any of the situations detailed below:

- Accidents or dangerous situations (to myself and others).
- Preoccupation with food.
- Attempts to control my eating.
- Loss of control of my eating and my behaviour.

Section II – Chaos

How has my inability to control my use of food, my behaviour and my feelings affected the following?

- My family and social life.
- My spiritual life (i.e. values, principles, beliefs, self respect).
- My work and financial life.
- My health.

8
Anorexia – the hunger strike

As I have said to you before I know that the paths into anorexia can be very different, but I want you to stick with me as I just outline a few:

6 I started starving after I changed schools at the age of fourteen, and I lost my best friend when I moved on. At the new school I just felt lonely. I also just didn't feel that I fitted in – that was when I homed in on my weight. Looking back I know that I wasn't overweight but I just hoped that if I looked different I would feel more acceptable. 9

6 It did all start off as a diet, or so I thought. My dad was travelling a lot and my mum used to get so lonely. I just started taking on too many of my mum's troubles. Part of me wanted someone to take care of me but there wasn't anyone, or so I thought. 9

6 I got really bad results in my 'O'levels. I felt that I had let everyone down. My parents tried to encourage me to go back to school to do re-takes but I took it that they were ashamed of me and I got so angry with them that I just couldn't talk to them any more. It was terrible, I just started to get obsessed with my weight and I lost sight of everything. I was eventually able to talk to my parents, and I did finally tell them what had really happened. 9

6 My dad started sexually abusing me when I was about nine years old. It started off really gradually, him coming into my room at night but always staying longer. He gave me extra pocket money and told me never to tell anyone what he did to

me in my pink bedroom. When I got older I realized that I had been the only one that this had happened to (I had a sister) and I started to wonder what was the matter with me, why had Dad singled me out. It was around this time that I started to 'diet' – I just didn't feel good enough to eat for. 〗

〖 Some other girls at school had anorexia. I sort of joined in. It felt like an exclusive club to join. I had never really felt that I belonged anywhere and all of a sudden we all got together and compared weights and talked about what we hadn't eaten. Later I started making myself sick and using laxatives. 〗

〖 You know everything in my life was so out of control. My mum and dad were splitting up and I just felt that I had no say or control in anything. I can't say it was a conscious decision to start starving. I just really found myself in the middle of it, and it used to make me feel really good and powerful. Then it just took me over. I got really scared, but I couldn't see a way out. 〗

〖 I used to be very overweight. I was teased at school and no one ever wanted to be my friend. I was put on a diet which I found really difficult to follow. Then I really got into it and, as the weight started to come off, I realized that I was becoming more popular. I got so used to dieting and getting lots of affirmation from people that I went completely overboard. I eventually became afraid to eat because I had the feeling that once I did I wouldn't be able to stop. 〗

I hope that these extracts can dispel the myth that all anorexics have been sexually abused or simply have what has been called the 'slimmers' disease'. All of these stories relate to young girls and women who resorted to starving themselves because they felt so badly about themselves. Just take a moment to think that the act of deliberately starving yourself, possibly vomiting, abusing laxatives and overexercising are hardly acts of self-love. These are acts which make you feel even worse about yourself. Just take a second to imagine how you would feel if someone was to catch you doing some of the things that you have to do to keep so thin. I know that you don't feel proud of what you do. I know you feel considerable shame, pain and embarrassment.

Some of those extracts are also cries from anorexics saying, 'Help, there is something wrong.' I can understand that you may feel that there is nothing else to do but to carry on with what you're doing but, believe me, there are other ways out of your problems. Others have felt that their lives were so out of control that they needed to bring some order into their lives. We all need to feel that we have some control over life but, if we don't, we could resort to fairly drastic measures to give us that feeling that we are still in the driving seat.

One thing that I know is so important to ask you is:

Why are you on hunger strike?

I know that you may not want to answer this question straight away but I am sure that you know the answer – and the answer is the key to getting you out of this trap once and for all.

I also want you to believe that:

Pushing food at you is not going to resolve anything long term.

Don't misunderstand me – you need food to live. I know that you cannot think straight while you are starving yourself, but I hope that you are sufficiently alert to hear what I am saying now. If you are not sufficiently alert then I want you to keep coming back to this chapter until you feel that you understand what I am saying to you.

If you are starving yourself, or bingeing and then vomiting there is something wrong. It does not mean that there is something wrong with you as an individual. I know that things must be pretty desperate if you are doing this, and I know that I cannot work a miracle through this book, but I do hope that if things don't change for you, you will consider finding someone to help you professionally. If you have already tried then think again if it did not work for you. Remember that when you have help you need to work as a team. No one can make you get well but there are plenty of people out there who can help you if you do 50 per cent of the work.

At the beginning of the book I mentioned the 'Food Plan' to you. Whatever you are going to do, you need to get back to eating food to fuel your body properly .I am not talking about getting you to put on lots of weight quickly but just eating sufficiently to increase your weight gently to a medically acceptable level. If you are seriously underweight you may need medical assistance in the beginning and you should be advised by a doctor; but remember, your recovery is not about being fattened up.

I also wonder how much fluid you have been drinking. Isn't it frightening when you can't even allow yourself a glass of water because you feel bloated? You and I know that water contains no calories and yet you will so often let yourself get completely dehydrated, which is so dangerous for you.

Assignment

I would like you to take some time and think about what you were like before all this began. I know that you will remember and I can understand that it is hard to look back and see yourself as you used to be. I imagine that you feel almost split in two between the girl that looks back and the one (who will be very weak at the moment) who wants to be well again. I want you to start to be aware of that other side of you. The side that you haven't been listening to for a very long time.

When you are ready I would also like you to think of writing your own 'Day in the Life' – you can look at Chapter 12 to see what other people have written. Remember that you don't have to show this to anyone – this is personal – but I want you to write it and then look at it when you are ready.

When you look at your 'Day in the Life' I want you to think of what all this has been costing you as a person. What has it felt like when you have woken up in the morning 'dying' to eat? It's OK, I know you can't admit this to everyone, but it is perfectly natural to crave food.

What has it been like to lose friendships and cope with the anxiety this has caused your family? When you are ready, I want you to consider that there might be another way for you to continue your life. It will be a life where you can talk to someone if you want to, and you can stop treating yourself so badly and start to take care of yourself by coming out of the isolation and start being 'good enough to eat for'.

Please get yourself a piece of paper and write down the costs of your anorexia. I know that anorexia might also have benefits for you, so divide the paper into two columns, the costs on one side, the benefits on the other. You will have to 'fight' that anorexic side of you to face the costs, but please get them written down.

I would finally like to make a bargain with you. You will have become an expert at keeping your weight down to a minimum. You are not going to lose that, so please don't be afraid that you are suddenly going to put on masses of weight. I would doubt that you would let that happen. Please take up the above suggestions. If they don't work for you, you would have lost nothing, if they do, you will make changes beyond your wildest dreams.

9

The hidden eating disorder

Exercise can become a dangerous addiction

I wonder how many people know how you really feel? We all judge people so much by their exterior. If you look good, i.e. slim, toned and fit, you tend to get admired and treated as if you shouldn't have a care in the world. You must be OK because you *look* it . . . but you know different. You know how *driven* you feel – the preoccupation with running, aerobic classes, getting to the gym, running your hand over your impossibly flat stomach and feeling guilty if you just once eat too much. But even more than that, it doesn't really matter how 'perfect' you look because it never quite changes the way you feel inside. It is hard to be trapped inside the perfect body when basically you just don't feel good about yourself.

Before we go any further, I am not suggesting that it isn't OK to look good, but what I am more interested in is you *feeling* as good as you look on the inside. If you get really honest it may be that you are really overexercising and using purging, laxatives or starvation to keep up this facade of 'Look I'm OK'. You see, the price of 'slim' gets higher and higher if this is happening. It is one thing to be naturally slim, and another to endanger your physical and mental well-being by vomiting starving or using laxatives.

You may also ask, 'What is the harm in me exercising?' The answer simply depends on how much you do – and how much it is costing you? I don't mean financially.

ARE YOU:-
● Preoccupied?

DO YOU FEEL:
● Anxious (if you can't exercise)?

DO YOU GIVE UP:
● Friends
● Social life
● Relationships
● Fun
in order to exercise?

Basically, is exercise getting in the way of leading a normal life? Exercise should be something that fits into normal living, not normal living being made to fit around exercise. This book is about finding a healthy balance. Take time to think if you have this with exercise.

As you will have read in the other chapters there are some people whose weight alters dramatically. Sometimes they are thin and sometimes overweight. Your weight may stay pretty constant – but you need to ask yourself how much time are you spending on keeping your weight down and how much is it costing you?

HOW MUCH:
1. Time do you spend thinking about what you can eat?
2. Time do you spend wishing that you could enjoy high-calorie foods?
3. Time do you spend feeling guilty if you have eaten more than you planned?
4. Variety is there in what you eat, or are you stuck in a low-calorie rut?
5. Have you noticed how your priorities have changed? How everything centres around food or avoiding it?

HOW LITTLE:
1. Do you spend on you, as a human being – not as a human doing?

2. Do you pay attention to people, places and things around you?
3. Time do you have for hobbies?
4. Time do you have to simply have fun?

Take some time to think about this. I also hope that those of you who believe: 'If only I could be thin and everything would be OK' take note that good feelings at the end of the day come from within. You are you, not 100 per cent what you look like. Shaping your life on, 'When I am thin . . . ' will always end in disappointment.

You see it's time to be good enough for who you are and to begin to accept yourself for how you are really built. If you have wide hips, then so be it. If they are naturally wide, you can't change them, but you can exude that air of 'this is me'. Why do so many women fall into the trap of believing that they have to have a particular type of figure? You need to stop doing that to yourself. Be an individual, but even more importantly be good to yourself and be healthy.

It's the same for men. If you are naturally thin, why feel that you are any less a man? Fine, if you want to be fit and healthy, that is one thing, but you don't need to walk around feeling bad about yourself.

10
Freedom from food

Learning to take responsibility

I know you can't really believe me when I say that there really can be freedom from food. What I mean is that it is possible to be free from:

Bingeing
Starving
Overeating
Overexercising
Purging

and also,

Obsession and preoccupation with food/eating/starving.

Throughout this book you will have heard me say, over and over again in many different ways, that diets are not the answer when you have an eating disorder, they simply become part of the problem. I have not asked you to go on a 'diet' – I have asked you to make some changes, and these need to be changes that become a daily routine for you. Through this, food becomes the fuel for your body, not a substance of abuse, and through this you gain the ultimate freedom which means that you don't have to think about food all the time – whether to eat, not eat, make up excuses. All these time-consuming crazy-making thoughts that have been part of your life for so long.

   In the introduction to the book I asked you to think about how you would describe your particular problem. Please refer back to this. How did you describe your problem? What did you say needed to change? What do you say to yourself about why this happens? It may be that now you have had time to read through this book, you may want to go back to these answers and add to what you have written.

Remember that these answers are for you. However, you may wish to share them with other people – friends, family, you doctor or therapist – it is entirely up to you. At this stage the most important thing is for you to be honest with yourself. When I use the word 'honest', I am not calling you a liar. I know from my own problems that I could never tell anyone what I was doing with alcohol. I was terrified by how people would react and what they would think of me. Start by being really honest with yourself and it will be this that will spur you on, especially if you can begin to glimpse that some of what you have been doing does make sense, but there is another way to deal and cope with how you feel about yourself – a more positive way.

The importance of having a plan

In Chapter 5 I asked you to consider writing a plan. I am sure that some of you immediately felt totally rebellious, but think again if you have not done this. It would be like setting out on a long journey, vaguely knowing where you are going but never planning the route or knowing which turnings to take. To put it simply, if you don't have a plan, how do you know where you are going? How do you know if you are going in the right direction? How do you know when you have got there? And most important of all, how do you congratulate yourself on succeeding by getting there.

I also want you to think of what picture you have in your mind of what changing would be like. You see you kid yourself that what you are doing at the moment is the best that it can ever be. So you immediately will think, 'He's asking me to do something different, so that will be terrible and I'm going to hate every minute of it and feel deprived'. Is it any wonder that you don't ever feel inspired and excited? Mention 'food plan', change, lose weight or gain weight and people hear 'deprivation'. Or for the anorexic it will be the word 'fat'. Why would anyone ever want to be 'deprived' or 'fattened up'? Neither of these sound remotely attractive, now, do they? Changing is not about these things being worse, believe me.

I would like you to think again very carefully about what you want. Yes, I know that some of it will be related to 'I want to look good', but I would also like you to think about you, your self-esteem, your confidence, how you relate to other people, what you enjoy doing in life, and what your ambitions are. Try to paint a picture that will motivate you. Think how we instinctively turn our faces to the sun because it feels so good. It should be the same when we change direction to a life that offers us so much more than we have had before. I can assure you that no one likes stepping into the darkness. Why ever would you?

All that I have done is give you some basic guidelines and suggestions. So if you get stuck in being rebellious ask yourself who you are really fighting. Don't you want to change? Or have you become so accustomed to feeling bad that it feels as if it is the only way to be? Look again at the plan. It is a plan for healthy eating and moving away from preoccupation. I am not telling you to be a vegetarian or to eat more vegetables, I am leaving that up to you, your tastes and also your common sense. Yes, I believe that deep down inside, you want to know some of what you should be eating, what foods are good for you and what aren't. (If you feel that you need more guidance then consult a good nutritionist or doctor – they are well equipped to give you sound advice.) If it seems difficult in the beginning, it will get better. It will get to be a new way of life. A new way of living.

Sticking to the plan

If you have written your plan, commenced it, but have

started to 'move the goalposts', STOP DOING THAT! I have worked with so many people who make a good start and immediately celebrate by going off their plan, and then wonder why things start going backwards. You have already discovered by now that you can't control your food intake when you move the goalposts around. Ask yourself who, or what, is in control and it will not be you.

If you have been in difficulties implementing this, take a good look at what has been happening. Use this information wisely. I know that you will feel really angry that you have this problem. So many people say, 'Why me? why can't I just be like my friend who can enjoy a box of chocolates and then leave them alone.' Acceptance of this problem is a major key that will unlock that door to freedom. I refer throughout this book to the 'Weight War', but the fight that is needed is not to fight the problem but to accept it and then fight to break free from it. Changing takes energy and enthusiasm, acceptance can be triggered by a good long reality check, and then knowing that you can change if you stop fighting the problem. It is not going to go away, but you can begin to tackle it in a very different way. You see, if your way of dealing with this had worked, you wouldn't be reading this book!

When I try to encourage someone who has difficulties, I ask them to tell me why they want things to change their relationship with food. It is at times like this that I feel a bit like a door-to-door salesman, except that when I open my suitcase there is nothing to show but their hopes and dreams. So I suppose I am asking you to take a bit of a leap in the dark with me. What have you got to lose? Isn't that a good question for you to ask yourself. Whatever your problem, all that you can lose is the pain, indignity, low self-worth, low confidence, health hazards, preoccupation and self-loathing. That is all that you have to lose, and if you really don't like what you find on the other side you can have back all that you have traded. You see you know how to binge, overeat, starve, purge, overexercise and be in control for periods of time. What you don't know is all that lies on the other side. If you don't try it, you will never know, and surely you deserve better than that. I can also say that once things start to change you won't want to let go.

So many anorexics fear that recovery from anorexia will bring them a life of being overweight. Once you have established a decent weight medically (and that does not entail having to be anything other than a weight where you will function in a healthy way) the food plan will really help.

Lots of people are amazed when I suggest this plan to an anorexic, but it is important to know that you don't have to run the risk of bingeing if you follow it. There is no room for bingeing if you are eating three meals a day, and you eat sufficiently at each meal. Eating too little, or starving for any period of time nearly always ends in bingeing because you simply get so hungry. You know that.

Many anorexics are treated by having to eat many thousands of calories a day, and may also need to be fed intravenously. All of this can be very necessary in acute cases because our bodies cannot survive without a certain amount of food. Once you are out of this danger area it shouldn't be necessary to continue to consume excess calories providing you maintain a 'healthy weight'. If you look at any medical weight chart you will see that weights exist in bands from the lowest to the highest acceptable weight. For an acceptable weight to be accurately calculated you need to be assessed properly, but the key point is to be at a weight where your body functions completely healthily, and none of this equals 'fat'. But, yes, it does equal listening to other people and freeing yourself from the trap of saying eating equals getting fat. The two don't go together. Food can equal being free and feeling good enough about yourself not to have to starve yourself. Again a key question to ask yourself is, 'What else am I not giving myself when I don't nourish my body with food?' Isn't it so boring just to always bring everything back to food, food, food. After all, there is so much more to you than what you eat, or what you don't eat.

Your thoughts should have lives and wills of their own. Just think for one second how much of a thief your eating disorder has been. Consider how you would feel if you came home

M FOOD** 103

and found that someone had broken into your home. It is so often a precious place where we would hope to feel safe and secure. We often surround ourselves with our favourite things or we save up and plan to buy something new or special for our homes. We also like to have people in our home who we like and trust. Stop there and think of your compulsive overeating, starving, bingeing and pre-occupation.

It's just as though one day (you probably can't quite remember when) you said goodbye to choice and lost your freedom. One day, when perhaps you weren't looking, someone got into your home and started to wreak havoc. Your story may even be that you opened the door and thought you were letting in a friend, but what you let in was a thief, a thief that steals freedom. It is time to shut that thief out.

11
The family affair

Your eating disorder involves people who care about you

Every week for the last ten years I have been working with families. These families have all included either a drug addict, an alcoholic, a person with an eating disorder, a compulsive exerciser, a compulsive spender, a gambler or a workaholic. Although the substances that each of these people use are different, the one thing that is most certainly the same is the effect on the family.

Everyone who comes into contact with you in one way or another will be affected by your eating disorder. It's easy for your friends to pull away from you and say that they don't want you around anymore, or they don't want you to go out with them. It is also easy for your employees to say that they don't want to work for you anymore, or for your boss to sack you and tell you that you are not doing your job properly because of your behaviour. But what about your family? What do they do? Not all of them can just shut the door on someone that they love, or walk away and leave you to destroy yourself. More often than not they choose the only way that they can see and that is to try to sort it out themselves.

You see this is what families do. They take care of each other. They are a system and they live within their own rules. Some families' rules are different from others, but generally the rule is that families will sort out their own problems and if there is something wrong it should be kept within the family and not discussed with other people. Families like to be seen as happy, functional systems. So a whole wall of pretence is built up around the problem. On the outside the family looks very happy and everything looks fine. Sons and daughters are getting on at school or in their careers, mum's happy, dad's happy – but behind this wall of pretence is unhappiness and confusion, anger and shame. The family don't know what is happening or what to do, so they have to set up some rules to survive within the chaos.

Stage one

Your eating disorder is the most important thing in your family's life. While you are obsessed with eating, undereating, inducing vomiting, etc. your family is obsessed with stopping you. If you are overeating they will be constantly putting you on a diet, telling you how you look and comparing you to your brothers and sisters or other people's wives or husbands. They will continually go on at you, asking you the same old questions, 'Why can't you be the same as everybody else?' 'Why don't you pull yourself together and stop being so greedy?' 'Why don't you eat more?' 'Why are you continually going to the bathroom for hours on end and making yourself sick?' 'Why are you hiding food and buying more than you need?' 'Why is food more important to you than me?' 'What have we done to make you behave like this?' What they may not directly ask is, 'What is *really* wrong?' and you are probably far from being able to answer.

You will feel constantly under attack from your family, but what else can you expect? You see, they don't know or understand what is going on. They can't believe that the little girl or boy who once had a healthy appetite is now totally out of control with eating, or the husband or wife who used to like food, is now obsessed with it. Look back in the book at what I've been saying. This behaviour doesn't arrive at a chronic stage, it slowly, progressively gets worse, and there is no healthy way to adapt to unhealthy behaviour.

Believe me, I understand that as you are reading this many

feelings will be brought up, but we have to face the fact of what is happening. We have to look at the reality of the effect that this is having on your family.

Mothers, fathers, sons and daughters always feel responsible when there is a major problem in the family. However, this problem is different isn't it? We're talking about something that everybody does, and has to do, and that is EAT. This is why it is so hard for people to understand about eating disorders. When someone is drinking too much, people can say, 'Oh he's got a drinking problem, he's an alcoholic, he needs to stop drinking.' When someone is using drugs, the same applies, 'He needs to stop using drugs.' Or exercise, 'Stop doing so much exercise.' Well, these statements may be fine for those other conditions, but not for food. If you stop eating, you'll die.

Of all the addictions that I treat, I really do believe that eating disorders are the worst, because you are constantly confronted with your problem every day of your life, and that is why throughout the book I harp on about taking responsibility and managing your food, instead of being managed by it. However, when you don't understand all this it is impossible, and you will feel as if you are going crazy. So imagine how your family feels when they see you behave like this and when they can't understand it. Are you getting the picture? Do you see what I mean?

The family starts to accept the unacceptable behaviour and enters into competition with the eating disorder, but although their goals lie in opposite directions, they are both playing the same crazy game. The eating disorder's use of food becomes the overriding concern within the family and no-one gets to talk about the real problems.

Stage two

This is how the family deals with the consequences of your eating disorder. Usually the first thing that the family will do is deny that there is a problem at all. I suppose this would be possible if the problem weren't so evident. What I mean is that a person with an eating disorder will wear what they are, e.g: if you are overeating you will be overweight, if you are undereating you will be underweight.

If you are inducing vomiting you will display physical symptoms, such as skin or teeth problems and the glands in your neck will be swollen, your lower face could take on a distorted shape. If you are abusing laxatives you will have internal problems, and it will be noticeable that you are constantly using the bathroom. A denial of the problem becomes a denial of reality, and when reality is denied only craziness can set in.

Imagine the scenario: two wives are talking to each other about a dinner party that one of them had a few days before. The one who gave the party says to the other:

'Gosh! Your Bill likes to eat a lot doesn't he?'

The other wife replies: 'Oh yes! He's always had a healthy appetite, I have to feed him very well.'

But what she isn't saying is that she was really angry with Bill and very embarrassed at the way he behaved because the party was a buffet dinner, and Bill practically ate everything that was on the table, he couldn't get enough on his plate and when he cleared his plate he still went back for more – but what can she say? How can she get through that denial. Just think about all the shame in this. How can her friend say to her:

'Tell me what's wrong? Why does he eat like that? Has he got a problem with food? Is he unhappy?'

You see she can't say these things because she will be met with the possible response:

'What do you mean? There's nothing wrong, he just likes his food, he's got a healthy appetite. What's wrong with that? Why are you making a big fuss about the way Bill eats? Has he upset you or done something wrong? Why are you asking me all these questions? If you don't want us to come to your house why don't you just say?'

This is so sad because before the dinner party Bill's wife said to him:

'Please don't eat so much tonight Bill, remember what you did the last time when you ate twice as much as anyone else. People are beginning to notice and I feel really embarrassed.'

Bill will probably respond with:

'Shut up! Mind your own business, why are you always nagging me about how much I eat? I'll eat as much as I want. If you didn't nag me so much I probably wouldn't eat so much. It's all your fault you're always telling me when I do something wrong. You're always telling me how fat I look. If you don't like me why do you stay with me?'

So Bill gives all his shame and out-of-control feelings back to his wife, and she stands there and takes it, but she feels so helpless and frightened because she can't see any way out, and at that point neither can Bill. So there you have the two main stays in a family that are frightened and confused and who give each other their shame. Neither one accepts it because they are not talking through what is really happening. Then it extends outside the family, because families don't like letting other people know what is going on. They don't want the neighbours to know that they are having problems, but then if the neighbours are like most they'll hear the arguments and shouting and see the bags of food being brought into the house.

Other children will be asking your children questions. 'Why is your daddy so big?' 'Why is your mummy so fat?' 'Why is your sister so thin? Why doesn't she eat anything? Doesn't your mummy feed her?' Your children, in turn, will make up excuses because they'll want to protect the secret, they won't want to be singled out.

Can you see what is happening, what is taking place, and how this behaviour is filtering right through your family.

When I'm giving lectures on addiction, I always use the concept of the family as a central heating system. You have the thermostat, the boiler, and the radiators placed around the home. Now if you think about it, the thermostat is usually the mother, who tries her best to keep the peace and to keep everything running smoothly within the family. The boiler is usually father. Now if the boiler breaks down, the thermostat will be totally unable to control what is happening, and so the radiators will be affected. In turn, if the thermostat breaks down, the boiler won't work properly and nor will the radiators.

Once there is addiction within the family it cannot function properly it can only dysfunction. The family will try every which way to survive because that's what families have to do. Whatever happens they have to stick together and try to look after each other, even though something is terribly wrong. This is not only painful for the person with the eating disorder, but for everybody in the family, as it affects everyone's behaviour.

For whatever the family try to do there is an underlining feeling of unhappiness, and where there is unhappiness there will be anger, guilt and blaming. More times than not someone or something will be scapegoated. It could be the husband, wife, children, job, colleagues, boss, marriage, etc. Anyone, anything or any situation could be blamed to try to deal with the feelings of worthlessness and guilt.

Stage three

This is when the family tries to rationalize what is totally irrational. Have you ever thought what it must be like for someone to be blamed for something that they don't understand or can't make any sense of? Can you see what is happening? The family begins to take on your unacceptable behaviour, and at the same time they try to rationalize it and make it all OK.

Imagine the scenario: the family sitting at the dinner

table, they are just coming to the end of their evening meal when one of the family leaves the table and goes upstairs to the bathroom. The rest of the family keep on eating without looking up, or without saying anything, even though they know that the person has gone to the bathroom to make themselves sick. They sit in silence whilst they all think the same thing .Maybe someone will say something to try and strike up a conversation, which will hopefully stop them all hearing the sounds of someone being sick upstairs. What sort of normality is this? Look at the picture. A family denying what is going on amongst them. Can you make sense of this? I can't.

Imagine another situation of a family sitting having dinner, with one member of the family missing. The missing person is upstairs refusing to eat, or if they are eating it will be the most minimal amount. The family again will carry on as if nothing is wrong. How real is this, how honest is it? This brings us to stage four.

Stage four

This is the family treading on egg shells around you, and you are in such emotional pain yourself that you can't handle your family's pain as well. So it goes on and on with everyone hoping that something is going to change and that one day soon the problem will go away. But the problem isn't going anywhere, it will just get worse because, as your addiction progresses, you will withdraw deeper and deeper into yourself because of the shame and guilt that you are feeling. Then the family will be looking at a shell, the remnants of what was once a healthy and loveable person. Can you imagine what that is like for the family? For them to watch the destruction of someone that they love, and no matter how much they say and do things or however much they try to please, cover up and tell lies, nothing changes – it just gets worse.

Can you even begin to imagine the pain that the family

experiences? I suppose you think that it's unrealistic of me to ask you to think about this, but I must ask you to start thinking about this because if you don't, Lord knows what will happen. If changes aren't made, your family will pull away as they won't be able to sustain this sort of behaviour. You may be thinking, 'I haven't got any of these problems, I'm not behaving in any way like this, my family aren't like this, what's he talking about?' Add a 'yet' on to that. You've come this far, so what makes you think that it won't get any worse? You are going to have to make some changes. You don't have any options left. You might think that you have, but I'm telling you that you haven't. You can deny what has been going on, but I'm not going to accept it because you and I both know how serious this is becoming and you must take responsibility.

The key lies with you. Once you start to get well, imagine the relief you'll feel when you take that first step to recovery. If you understand nothing else in this chapter, please understand that you are not the only one involved in this.

If you are emotionally in pain, then so are your family. Why wouldn't they be? They love and care for you. The rules have to change, they must be changed for healthier ones. Can your family survive this? I believe they can, but you must take the first step – you hold the key – but you also hold the key to the destruction of your family. If you are going to do something about your eating disorder, you have the capacity to survive – but if you don't, the only end is unhappiness and the destruction of yourself and then your family.

It is all in your hands – you are in charge – you have the power to change the rules that your family has set up. How much do you love your family? Do you love them enough to take a big step back and look at what is going on? Or if you feel that you can't, why don't you ask them? Maybe show them this book, point out this chapter, and see how much they identify themselves with it.

Now I'm asking you to take some risks aren't I? Am I asking too much of a commitment? It's getting late in the day so you've got to take some action. We're talking about salvaging a relationship here. You've got to use every option that you can.

I suggest that you read this chapter again, because the one thing that you've got to understand is that you will lose people around you if this behaviour continues. I personally know what that is like, and I've no wish for you to lose what I lost. If you have any doubts about what I've just said, ask yourself this question: 'What do you offer your family in terms of happiness, security and fulfilment?'

Don't put this book down. You've got this far and you have to look at the pain before you can get into recovery. You have the strength. You can survive, but you need to take responsibility. It's your choice. You are worth this and so are your family.

12
A day in the life of . . .

This chapter really belongs to some of the people who I've worked with in the last few years. They have very kindly agreed to write 'a day in the life' for me. I asked them to do this because I believe that it is really important that you hear from some other people what their eating disorders have done to them. I'd like you to read these stories that are written by people who have really been in the depths of despair with their eating, but have made a decision to come back and make some very positive changes to lead a normal life.

While you are reading these stories you may think, 'But I'm not as bad as this, Beechy, I haven't had these consequences, I haven't done these things, I've never eaten like that.' Add a 'yet', because if you look back over your eating patterns you will see how they have progressed this far and there is simply no reason why you won't carry on going down hill if you don't make some changes.

I am very happy to say that the people who have written these stories are very much alive and well today. They are all in recovery from their eating disorders and living lives of happiness and fulfilment.

Jenny

❛ The house is clean, the answerphone is on, the post has been dealt with. I am showered and clean. Clean that is on the outside, inside there's a seething mass of deceit, anger, fear and loneliness. I've put myself in exile, I move among people less and less often these days. I move among them but am apart from them. I can't let anyone know the despair, rage and frustrating bewilderment which has consumed me – I'm so ashamed, I can't control my behaviour. I am very civil, very sharp and very moody. I make sure that no one gets close to me and discovers my dreadful secret. I make them uneasy.

Some secret – I look in the mirror, or rather I look to check that my mascara is not smudged. I don't look at 'me' anymore. The woman reflected back is very pale, a slight sheen of sweat, manic blank eyes look back at me – I don't know her, she looks menacing and haunted, hope has died in there. I don't know her but she is me. I am scared of her. Scared of the barely concealed madness. I don't really dress anymore, it's a case of camouflage – dark colours – nothing fitted because nothing fits now anyway. I don't look at my body, it disgusts me. I keep 'it' clean – dark clothes, clean, anonymous – as invisible as an insane fat woman can be.

I walk purposefully to the supermarket, isolated in my mania. Crazy fairy tales playing in my head. A secret tight smile on my mouth. I am single minded, the demons have to be appeased. I don't want to run into anyone I know, to be interrupted or delayed. It's urgent, it must be done right now. I don't want questions. I don't want to feign polite interest in someone else's tedious life. The imagery in my head is so much more appealing. A white knight on a charger, a prize, something, someone as yet unknown to transform my life. I also re-run past arguments in my head to feel the unfairness, to win the arguments I lost, to hurt the people who mistreated me – revenge, hatred, fantasy, past and future but rarely the present.

I don't meet anyone along the way and for once the supermarket isn't too crowded. I hate crowds. I get a trolley, I know the aisles. My favourite, the ready meals and delicatessen. Scotch eggs, rollmops, garlic for the nice thick fatty half shoulder of lamb, large pack of frankfurters, mint sauce, potatoes, a pineapple, a lasagne. It vaguely occurs to me that I'm trying to kill myself with cholesterol. Heart disease features in my father's family. My parents are dead and I don't get on with the rest of my family, I'm too weird and too elusive. I don't belong – so be it.

Food, my comfort, my obsession and my tormentor. Half a pound of butter, a packet of stuffing, gravy granules, quiche, ham slices and black pudding. I see a girl I went to school with push her child past in a trolley – boring cow – she has a child, a family, a home, she's so nice – I loathe her. Luckily she doesn't see me. I would have had to lie about friends coming for dinner to explain all the stuff in my trolley. Lies come easily, spontaneously, easier to live with than the truth. No friends, deep deep loneliness, fear, and I can't see a way out. I've tried, believe me, I've tried. Diets, clubs, gyms, courses, socializing and forcing friendliness – but I fail, I always fail, I'm in too deep, I'm beyond reach. This is my experience, not really a life and I'll be relieved when it stops. I can't be bothered to kill myself, I tried that and failed, so now I drag my bloated carcass along in tormented apathy. A waste.

Trolley full, pulse rate up, impatience at the checkout. Pay by card as I don't want to see just how much this blow out is costing. It also leaves me money for a taxi. It'll be quicker to get home, less chance of being seen with all the bags of food. Quicker to start, to let loose. Food is the focus of all my waking hours.

Bags on the kitchen floor, I cram Scotch eggs in my mouth while I'm pushing garlic cloves into the lamb. I pick at cheese and grapes while I peel and boil the potatoes – I put the potatoes in to roast with the lamb. I take a tray of goodies (quiche, fruit, crisps) into the lounge to graze through.

I'll watch a film in delicious anticipation of the feast to come – a fragrant hot filling family roast, but there's no family, just me, and I don't even belong to me. Satisfaction will be short lived, it always is, and I'll do it again in a few days' time. I hate it, but I can't stop it. I feel so sick of food, of life, of everything. The answerphone is on but no one has rung. I think even God's forgotten about me. There's a raging scream in my head but my mouth is full of food and no sound comes out. **9**

Sarah

6 The alarm clock sounds and my heart groans at the thought of making it through another day. My head aches from last night's tears. The biggest dread is climbing into something to wear today. After all that ceaseless eating, will there be anything in the wardrobe that I can squeeze into? Underwear is the most uncomfortable clothing of all as none of it fits properly and pulls at my flab all day.

Can I make today different? Last night I vowed that today would be the start of my slim life – no more bingeing, no more vomiting and an end to all the self-hatred I feel.

I manage breakfast quite well. Two slices of toast and plenty of coffee. Nine o'clock comes and the hunger begins. I try to think of all the reasons why I must not eat:

- My poor children having a nineteen-stone mother.
- My poor husband. How embarrassed he must be of me.
- The look on my friend's face when I saw her recently. She did her best to disown me. How ashamed I felt.
- So that my sister-in-law will not make a big scene ensuring that I sit in the front seat of the car and all the slim members of the family sit in the back.

The shame I feel now leads me towards the fridge. I will just have two more slices of bread. What harm could that do? Ten minutes later I register that I have devoured six more slices without even tasting them. It reminds me of our family dog who used to swallow food without it touching the sides of his throat.

'Well, you have really blown it for today, Sarah.'

An odd sort of excitement grows inside me as I plan a trip to the supermarket for all my favourite forbidden foods. There will be no one at home to disturb me – perhaps that diet can wait until tomorrow. After all, what is twenty-four hours out of a lifetime?

Once I am in the supermarket I reach for all my binge foods. These consist of crisps, peanuts, doughnuts, battenburg cake, meringues with fresh cream, salami, chocolate-covered nuts and raisins, fruit and nut chocolate, Toblerone and a large packet of Mars bars. The last thing is always carbonated water and ice-cream. These are the two necessities for throwing up.

I dash home munching the nuts and raisins as I drive. I couldn't possibly wait until I got home.

Once I am safely ensconced at home I sit myself down on the familiar sofa in my kitchen. I proceed to eat solidly. I am totally absorbed and would kill anyone who disturbed me or got in the way.

Feeling full, I reach for the mineral water and guzzle it straight from the bottle. Just two bowls of ice-cream and I should be ready.

At this point I feel violently sick. After tying back my hair I lift the loo seat and stick my fingers down my throat. Up comes a lot of food. The reason I am a failed bulimic is that I only ever throw up enough food to make room for more. If I was better at it I wouldn't be so obese.

An hour passes and I am wondering what to have for lunch. Something hot would be nice but I can't face cooking. I would die for a McDonald's.

Within half an hour I am back at home with two Big Macs, two large fries, and two apple pies. I am convinced that the waitress knew that it was all for me.

I gobble my way through lunch and by now feel far too sleepy and exhausted to even contemplate vomiting.

The telephone wakes me and it is my husband encouraging me to play tennis with him this evening – panic – I couldn't put one leg in front of the other after all this food, and I certainly couldn't parade around in any clothes that would be suitable for tennis.

'No thanks, darling. I have promised Maureen the night off and can't leave the children.'

After our conversation I realise how often I use the children as an excuse.

At three o'clock I set off to collect the children from school. A couple of fresh croissants would be nice to keep me going. I buy four and pull at them out of the bag as I drive. I am just finishing the last one as I park outside the school. There is a knock at the car window and I open it as I swiftly brush crumbs off my shelf-like chest.

'I do hope you don't mind me asking, Sarah, but where on earth do you buy your clothes? I have got a very fat friend from India staying and we can't find any clothes big enough.'

I smile cheerfully, although I am dying inside.

'Of course, I couldn't mind less.'

I immediately feel like an elephant. Every crumb of food that I have eaten today comes into my head, and all around me. I feel as though this tactless woman can see it and that I am nothing but a greedy, useless pig.

My reaction to this awful experience starts with my snapping impatiently at the children all the way home. As soon as we arrive home I make straight for the sanctuary of my bathroom. I try desperately to throw up again but without much success.

'I would rather be dead than doing this. How can I end it all?'

It is now seven o'clock and the children are in bed. If I hadn't had such a lousy day food-wise I would have had time to read to them. When I am in the food I can think of nothing else and I certainly don't want the children around me.

I make my excuses to Maureen the au pair and make my last journey out to the corner shop. Just a few chocolates and sweets to finish up with. I buy two Twix and two Mars bars and head home.

As soon as I get in the front door I go straight to the sitting room and hide the sweets behind one of the chairs. Knowing that the food is hidden there feels safe.

My husband comes back from work as I am preparing supper. We talk about the day and I paint a totally false picture. We sit down and eat lamb chops, baked potato and peas, followed by cheese and fruit. He eats hungrily saying that he only had time for an apple for lunch. It is so unfair. Why can't I forget to eat? Why can't I control what I eat? Ever since I was a six-year-old child and I was granted a wish it was always that I might forget about food and wanting to eat it all the time.

Just before I go upstairs for my bath, I sit in darkness in the sitting room finishing the rest of my sweets. As I bathe I look at my body in disgust. The bath feels so small tonight. All around me in the bathroom I see disapproving faces looking down at me. I climb into bed tearfully and pray, 'Please God, make tomorrow be better.'

JULY 1994

As I look back at the way my life was I feel deep sadness for the person I had become. Over the past two years since I 'cleaned up' I have realized that my life before was only ever food. The sadness is for the lost years when I was gripped by the all-consuming disease of overeating. Thirty years of my life were dominated by that beast.

When the beast rears it's ugly head today I cope with it in a different way. I have learnt to talk about my feelings of self-hatred, low self-esteem, anxiety, inadequacy, jealousy, anger and sadness. I have also learned, slowly, to experience good feelings.

The physical change has come as a result of the way I live my life today. I have lost seven stone and maintained the loss. In the past I reckon I lost and gained forty stone. I feel confident that I will attain a normal weight as my recovery continues. I can accept that the illness of overeating will be on my shoulder waiting to kick in for the rest of my life.

I love myself today. I value my individuality and sensitivity. I no longer function solely as a wife, mother, sister or daughter but as me, a person in my own right. There is no need to hide behind my children to avoid life.

I play tennis and swim regularly with diminishing hang-ups. Last summer I won a tennis tournament.

Religion has never featured strongly in my life but I am sure that someone is looking after me.

I enjoy life now. There are days when all I can think of is food, but these are now outweighed by the easier days. I am learning to look at the reasons behind why I want to numb out with food. Gone are those suicidal feelings that frightened me so much.

Life is never going to be easy, but one day at a time, one meal at a time, I feel able to face it and this is a gift that I thank God for, and especially Beechy. It was Beechy who helped me to understand the disease and who made me believe that I am not a fat, greedy, hopeless person who can't keep her nose out of the fridge. 〉

Gillian

❛ My name is Gillian and I have been bulimic for five years now.

It all started when my father died. I felt lost and alone and the bulimia was my friend. Little did I know then that it was to become my worst enemy.

When I wake up in the morning my first thought is, 'How much do I weigh?' That is followed by a visit to the bathroom to jump on the scales. The result just devastates me, even if I have only put on one pound, I am repulsed by myself. This always results in about twenty laxatives being taken before breakfast. Then, due to the fact I've taken laxatives, breakfast is a pigout. Anything I have in the fridge (I always have lots of food) bread, butter, pasta, cheese and crisps. Then the huge pangs of guilt arrive – 'What have I done.' Depending on how much I've eaten, I make myself sick and then weigh myself again.

It is then time for work. I work for myself so it is very easy to be in control of buying food for binges and laxatives. I never leave the house without checking that I have enough laxatives for the day.

Quite often I buy something to eat on the way to work, e.g. a packet of biscuits. Work is fine, except that I am always trying to work out how I am going to get out to lunch – which is mad as I will only binge and take about 10-20 laxatives.

While I am driving around in the car I will stop at every chemist and buy laxatives to keep my supply up. On the way home I'll stop and buy some food, even if I'd planned to go out. I'll eat it as soon as I get home and then be sick or take laxatives and feel so guilty and ashamed of myself that I'll phone the person who I was going out with and somehow get out of it. I am more lonely than ever.

Before going to bed at night I'll take another 20 laxatives and pray that in the morning I'll be thin.

I weigh 7 stone and I'm 5 ft 8 in, with small bones. Food to me is evil and I will do anything in my power to get rid of it. I once even thought about taking a carving knife to my thighs.

Bulimia has ruined the last five years. It is not going to ruin the rest of my life. 〉

Vanessa

❝ I open my eyes in the morning, feeling hung over from the day before. Negative feelings come rushing back – self-hatred and guilt for having yet again succumbed to my disease of bulimia.

My face is puffy, my throat is sore. I feel bloated and nauseous. All as a result of the vicious cycle that is bingeing and throwing up, which I have been unable to break.

I think to myself, 'I will try to be good today,' meaning that I will try to control my food and eat healthily in order to lose weight and become the slender, successful model I once was prior to my illness.

So I get up, try to smile at my sad reflection in the mirror and go to the kitchen to make myself a cup of coffee. I do not quite know what I will be doing today. I cannot go to the agency, being too overweight to go to castings, so, yet again, I am attempting my all too familiar mission: go on a diet, take control.

I therefore decide to go to my local gym in order to burn up some calories. I cycle like a maniac for an hour, run for half an hour and do some weights, and while I am sweating, I fantasize about my future success and recovered slenderness. I take a shower, look at my watch: time for lunch. I head towards Marks and Spencer where I buy a couple of their crunchy coleslaw salads, no dressing of course. I am starting to feel quite optimistic: I have been to the gym, I am having a low-cal lunch. Perhaps I will be able to make it today.

Lunch is over. I light up a cigarette and make myself another cup of coffee. What shall I do next? I pick up a book on positive thinking to try to control my flow of negative thoughts and feelings, read for a while and then BANG! I start feeling hungry. What can I do? My ill thinking process begins: I have been good so far, I have burned up about 500Kcal at the gym, no breakfast and a salad for lunch, perhaps I can eat something. I try to control my feeling of hunger, light up a cigarette, make myself another cup of coffee and try to read some more of my book – but the feeling comes back even stronger. I *have* to eat something.

My disease had taken over now and I am it's slave. Like a robot, I grab my wallet and my keys. I walk down the stairs, my head is on automatic mode. I go to the local shop and buy enough food to go on what I call a 'tastebud adventure': sweet, salty, crunchy, soft. All my morning resolutions, my renewed mission are long forgotten. My illness, on the other hand, has completely taken me over, very much like the beast in the movie *Alien*. Having bought my binge food, I go back to my room and lay everything on my bed. What shall I have first? For the few minutes that my 'tastebud adventure' lasts, I am appreciating every flavour, texture, wanting to experience them over and over and to never end. When there is no food left, the realization of what I have just done is too overwhelming. How could I let myself do this? What happened to all my good intentions? I won't be losing weight today now. When will I be able to go back to my agency and start working again?

I am now feeling full of despair and anger, I hate myself. *I hate myself!*

There is no way I am going to let myself digest this food. I have got to get rid of it and there is only one way to do this!

I go to the kitchen, grab my red bucket, a carrier bag which I place in the bucket. I go to my bedroom, grab my toothbrush and stick it down my throat. I have to bring up everything so that all I have eaten won't count and won't spoil my 'good' first day. The whole procedure is so exhausting.

Tears are running down my red puffy face. I keep pressing my toothbrush against the back of my tongue until I reach a state of nausea and watch sadly the carrier bag fill up slowly. I feel sad, so so sad.

I then close the plastic bag and take it down to the big rubbish bin. I try to cheer myself up again. Comfort myself thinking: it's OK, tomorrow is another day, I will be good tomorrow. **)**

Michael

(I wake up before the alarm. I groan inwardly and hold my bulging stomach – God do I feel ill! I wonder how many men are waking up this morning feeling as ill as I am. I expect they will have hangovers from something else – not food. I try to move quietly so as not to disturb Jane. I like to get to the bathroom first in the morning and wait for 'nature to take its course' as it does every morning with a vengeance.

I go into the bathroom and close and lock the door. I don't want her to walk in unexpectedly. I sit down and look again at my huge belly which is so solid I wonder how it doesn't just rip. Last night was one of many 'bad nights'. I was OK during the day but on the way home I just felt really fed up with myself.

I stopped at the Chinese and ordered a meal for three people. Barbecue spare ribs, chicken and cashew nuts, fried rice, king prawns and something else. The people in there know me so well.

I made my usual pretence that my wife and I had a friend coming for supper unexpectedly. (If only they knew.) Sometimes I think they do know and they always give me the impression that they think, 'He shouldn't be eating this sort of food – he needs to be on a diet.'

Once outside the takeaway, I walked quickly towards my car. The sense of excitement was almost too much. I got into the car and decided to drive to a road nearby where I would be able to eat without so many people going past but, as usual, I couldn't wait and ripped the hot damp top off the ribs and began eating whilst I was driving. One of these days I am going to get stopped. It is my nightmare. I could just imagine the jokes at work 'What, stopped for being fat in charge of a vehicle!'

Once in the sidestreet I stopped and continued stuffing the food into my mouth. The sauces ran down the corners of my mouth and I just wiped them away with the back of my hand. The food was still so hot that it burned my mouth but nothing stopped my wanting to cram that food into my mouth until it was all gone. I was, as usual totally unaware of the taste of the food but excited at getting closer and closer to that 'full feeling'. My heart pounded as I scooped more hot food in my fingers and stuffed it in. Once it was over I felt calmed for a few minutes and then the reality of what I had just done yet again hit me. Damn, I thought, why does this keep happening. What is wrong with me? I suddenly realized the time and knew that Jane would be waiting for me. I wiped my hands and face and drove off. I knew that my concentration was bad and I kept having to really jump on the brakes when cars in front slowed down when I wasn't expecting them to.

I dwell on this for a few minutes. After all, last night was not so different to all the times I have visited the takeaway on the way home and then sat down to a meal with Jane. My heart always sinks as she has prepared yet another low-caloried enticing meal – if only she knew? I have perfected the art (or so I think) of subterfuge – she simply cannot understand why I am so huge. I on the other hand feel rotten that I just lie and lie. But I can't tell her, she would be so disgusted. After supper we watched TV for a while and she went to bed. I always stay down to lock up. When I knew she was safely upstairs I went to the cocktail cabinet where we keep the peanuts and After Eights. I was sure she had forgotten that we still had some. I grabbed them and ate them whilst walking around switching things off and going to the back door to lock it. Thank heavens! I remembered they were there – I hate being caught without anything and Jane is so careful about what she keeps in the house. What a joke. I know that I have just got bigger and bigger.

I know that my size more than literally has come between Jane and me. If she even mentions my size I just get so uncontrollably rageful. The shame when she tries to delicately bring up the subject is so enormous. The words 'weight' and 'fat' are synonymous with me being a total failure. I inwardly cringe and feel all the self-disgust and fear. I ask myself time and time again, 'Why don't I stop?' 'Why do I risk my marriage?' I am sure that Jane finds me physically repellent and, quite frankly, there are times that I just can't be intimate with her – I feel like a lump not a man or a human being.

I don't know how my system copes – I feel really unwell and uncomfortable in the bathroom but know I will feel better once I go to the toilet. Yet again I have terrible wind. I feel disgusting and would be so ashamed if anyone could hear or see what happens every time I binge. The pain in my stomach is terrible but it always is – I feel resigned to it as I do to my terrible morning ritual. When I am finished I have to keep flushing the toilet – it just won't all go down. This is when I feel absolute shame. Once I have finished flushing the loo I grab the air freshener. I spray it as much for my benefit as Jane's. I also turn down the radio to a quieter level and feel that I can now shower and get ready for work. I turn the water on and stand under the jets. I look down and see my enormous girth and my feet protruding – my doctor has said that I am just stupid to weigh the 20 stones that I do. I am only 27 years old and I can't run upstairs without feeling ill and I can't go on a summer holiday with Jane and feel good on a beach. I see people look at us and think, 'What is she doing with him?' Loads of people keep saying 'you would be so good looking if you lost the weight', and yes I can remember how I looked at 15 stones, but that was some time ago.

I have always struggled with my weight. My Mum put me on loads of diets and I just felt so stupid. Boys shouldn't be on diets – I was teased at school for being fat and then teased for not eating sweets when I was on one of my diets. In the end I just became the butt of people's jokes and that way I became popular. I pretended that I was so hard that you could just tease and tease me and it wouldn't make any difference. If only they knew how I felt inside – but a few Mars bars and some bags of crisps and I would just forget for a while.

Jane's banging on the door. She is wondering why I have locked the door. I jump out of the shower and wrap a towel around myself before I open the door – these days I just hate her seeing me naked. As she walks past she pats my stomach and that makes me feel really angry. Perhaps today I can make a start. **9**

Jean

6 Jean, time to get up, it's 10 a.m.'

'OK, Mum, I'm up already.'

'Do you want breakfast Jean?'

'No thanks, just a coffee, Mum.'

As I heave myself out of bed, I catch a glimpse of my repulsive body in the mirror. I must remember to tell Dad to move it out of my room.

I want something to eat, maybe I'll just have two pieces of toast. As I ask Mum for the toast I think, 'I must get rid of the sweet wrappers from last night.' Stuffing everything into a carrier bag and turning the empty boxes of chocolates inside out so that nobody can see what they are, I hide the bag in my wardrobe. I'll get rid of it when Mum and Dad aren't around.

Whilst sitting down for breakfast no one speaks, but I can tell what they are going to ask in a minute, 'Why don't you start a diet?' or, 'How's your weight going?'

Sure enough, Mum says, 'How's the diet going?' Well, why should she ask anything different these days, after all, it's all we ever talk about?

'Fine,' I say and leave the table to go and get dressed.

As Mum drives me to work I'm thinking to myself, 'What can I have for lunch that isn't fattening? I know, just a sandwich with ham is fine,' but I fantasize about eating doorstep sandwiches filled with bacon and egg. I tell myself, 'No Jean, you're on a diet.'

Struggling out of the car outside work Mum says, 'Jean, try to be good with your diet today.'

'Get lost,' I reply and slam the car door. That's it, I've had it, I'll show her who's going to be good!

It's only 8.10 a.m. so I go into a sweet shop and buy three bags of crisps, two packets of mini digestives and a can of diet Sprite, after all I am on a diet. Then I go straight to work and into the toilet and eat the lot. Soon the other staff start to arrive. Thank God they didn't catch me!

At about 10 a.m. Natalie asks if anyone wants breakfast, 'Yes please,' I say, 'Can I have an avocado and bacon sandwich on brown, a bag of crisps, two cheese straws and a can of diet Sprite?'

Ten-fifteen comes and she's still not back; God she gets on my nerves. I'm hungry! With that she enters the office. 'I'll have mine now, Natalie, I haven't eaten since last night,' I say. I eat what she's brought me in a few minutes and look at my watch to see when lunch is, only one-and-a-half hours away. Every five minutes I look to see what the time is because I want my lunch.

Great, lunch time. I fly out of the office into the bakers and I buy one avocado and bacon sandwich, four cheese straws, one sausage roll, three lemon iced buns, two cherry bakewell tarts, one bag of crisps and finally one can of diet Sprite – telling the lady serving me that it's one of the girl's birthdays at work. That's why I'm buying so many cakes.

Taking this outside I sit in the park on my own making sure nobody can see me. I scoff the lot and hurry back to the office. Before I go in I buy a Snickers, two Cadbury's Cream Eggs and a packet of mints for myself to eat at work. Back in the office I start to feel tired looking at the computer and wish it was home time. Just then, Mike comes in and gives us all an ice-cream; that was a nice surprise, just what I need to get through the afternoon as I was feeling hungry again.

Five p.m. strikes and I hurry out of the door and buy a half pound of Roses, four half pound bags of chocolate raisins, milk gums, sherbert lemons, liquorice allsorts along with two Dove ice-creams, four bags of crisps and two cans of diet Sprite. While I'm standing in the queue I see the marshmallows, two for the price of one, I pick up two bags, can't miss a bargain. On no, it's the same guy who served me last night, I hope he doesn't recognize me. As I get to the front of the queue he smiles at me, I bet he knows all the sweets are for me, but anyway, I say they're for my cousins who are coming over tonight. I pay £9.67 and leave in a fluster. On my way to the taxi that takes me home I buy a loaf of granary bread to have as well.

I hate getting into the taxi, I'm sure the driver can see all the food in my bag. I get really embarrassed about it. Never mind, I just think of getting home and hope that Mum and Dad aren't in.

Great, they're not in. I rush upstairs and go straight to the bath-room and strip down to my knickers and bra and sit in the bath-room eating the Dove ice-cream when I hear Mum and Dad come in. Oh no! I'd better hurry up and hide the food and wrappers before they come upstairs.

Mum calls out to me, 'Jean, are you home?'

'Yes,' I reply, 'I'll be down in a minute.'

Quickly, I gather my clothes and the wrappers and rush into my room and hide everything. The ice-cream has melted into my skirt so I suck it off and eat it, after all you can't waste food.

I go downstairs and find Mum already preparing the dinner, she asks, 'How've you been doing with the food?'

'Really good,' I lie, 'I'm hungry now though.'

'It won't be long,' she says, 'We're having pasta.'

Dinner comes and goes really quickly because I'm dreaming of my food upstairs waiting for me, but I can't go up too early or they'll know what I'm doing.

Mum and Dad don't talk much, we just watch TV, but at 9.00 p.m. I have to go upstairs, I need to eat as I'm hungry, so I go off to bed.

Out come my treats for the night. As I sit on my bed I'm careful not to make a noise as I don't want Mum and Dad to hear what I'm doing. So quickly, but quietly, I start ramming food down my throat, at one point I lie down as I can't get any more in, but by lying down I make more room.

At about 9.30 p.m. I'm finishing the last slice of bread when the tears start to roll down my cheeks and I say softly to myself, 'Oh well! You didn't stick to a diet today, as usual you just ate all day.' I can now feel the tears rolling over the rolls of fat that form my chin. As I fall asleep I am saying to myself, 'Maybe tomorrow I'll start again, maybe it will be different.'

1994

Four years on, and my life has completely changed with the help of Beechy and the OA (Overeaters Anonymous) fellowship. I entered treatment in August 1990, not knowing exactly how much my life was about to change. Beechy was the first person to confront me and say, 'It's OK Jean, you have a disease. It's not your fault.' He also told me I would never have to go on a diet again. What a relief that was – but how? I thought – what do I have to do? I learnt to start eating properly which for me means three healthy meals a day and to avoid sugar, not once did anyone suggest salad and cottage cheese.

At once my weight started to drop. Not too much or too little. I now maintain over a ten-stone weight loss which has changed my physical life completely. At last I can go to the cinema without worrying if I will fit in the seat. I regularly go on holiday and don't panic about doing the seat belt up on the plane. I have recently overcome my fear of horses and started riding lessons along with cycling and swimming three times a week.

I live on my own in a flat with my kitten May. I don't panic or worry if I am going to be attacked at night. I have cupboards that have shelves with food on, rather than being bare. I have friends who love me just the way I am. They understand and listen to me when I am going through a rough time and they also share the good times with me. I now feel part of my natural family after feeling on the outside for so long. My parents love and understand me and we are able to say we love each other without running out of the room.

For myself I am learning to give myself all the things I have missed for so long. I tell myself how valuable I am and I give love to myself. I may buy a teddy bear for myself or go out with friends or sometimes I lie down, put on some soft music, and think of all the good things in my life. I am no longer in fear of waking up and wondering where my next mouthful of food will come from. I still have days when I think about food, but if I do, I phone someone or pray about it.

This September I am going to college to start an access course to do a degree in social work. This is a challenge for me as I left school with no qualifications worth mentioning. Well, now I am going back and can't wait to have that second chance. Like everything about my life, I have been given a second chance to be happy and take risks by fulfilling all my dreams.

Beechy is a very special person to me, not only as a therapist, but a friend who I respect and love very much. I can only finish by saying thank God I am abstinent *today!* 〉

Kate

〈 I wake up feeling groggy and hoping it's not too early, then there's not too much of the day to fill. First thoughts are, 'What did I eat yesterday?' Quick recall, managed to eat nothing until four and then . . . Oh damn! It started with that box of my favourite biscuits. I thought that they'd be OK providing I ate nothing else – but then I ended up with a large baked potato, covered in greasy Cheddar cheese and a jar of mayonnaise, convincing myself all the while that I needed something healthy and cheese is a good source of protein. I had to have the mayonnaise because anything without mayonnaise is like having bread without butter – it just isn't feasible.

Slowly I remember the evening watching telly and then the party at John's . . . suddenly a cramping in my stomach reminds me of the thirty laxatives I took. I rush to the bathroom. Good, get it all out. Back to bed. Yes, that party – Oh Jesus, it was awful. I spent the whole evening waiting for Jason to talk to me. In fact he seemed to be talking or rather chatting up everyone except me. God I felt so fat – holding my stomach in all evening and trying to rid myself of the guilt about those biscuits.

Eventually at the end of the evening Jason threw a few words in my direction. I'm mad about him, but he doesn't treat me well, or am I imagining it. Is this how men are? Jason and Christian go off for a strictly men's only evening. 'To pick up girls?', I enquire. He laughs. I laugh back – 'Go for it.' I reply. What a performance. I die inside.

Christian phoned me at 4 a.m. He wanted to come over and cook breakfast, he's coked up to the eyeballs. 'No,' I say. The laxatives have already taken effect and the idea of food seems strangely horrible. How I wish it was like this always. I go back to sleep.

A new day begins. A day I won't eat, starve myself and look beautiful. In two months I could lose two stone! I remember Jane losing eight pounds in a week. If she can do it so can I. Thinness is all. Then I will be happy.

I run a bath and climb in. damn, that cellulite – those hips and my bottom. Great wedges of fat everywhere. It seems so permanent, so solid, so immovable. God I hate it! It's to blame for all my misery.

I wander to the kitchen. My cupboards and fridge are always empty – then I won't eat. I search everywhere just checking. I find a large sliced loaf that I'd bought yesterday for Jason. I knew it was there as I also knew that a pat of butter and a jar of jam are also there. Jason hadn't touched it. I eat the whole loaf, all the butter and most of the jam. Funny I only meant to eat one slice. God I hope the laxatives are still working. Once I start eating toast I can't stop. Pieces disappear down my throat with practiced ease. I must stop — just one more slice. I chew it and spit it out – why bother. God I feel awful. Suicidal in fact, but I just want more. I find a bit half chewed and eat it. Is this what I'm reduced to? I will not cry – I never cry – I can't remember the last time I did.

Lunch at my mother's. I won't eat. I've decided to get drunk and smoke instead. The wine makes me hungry. God I need food to soak up all this alcohol. I sneak to the kitchen under the pretext of making a coffee. There are huge slices of greasy quiche, salad and a fish pie. I finish the entire dish of pie and ram slices of quiche into my mouth. Quite a good mix – it tastes divine, but after a few mouthfuls I don't taste, I just eat – fast, furiously and uncontrollably – I might be caught. I load a bowl with fruit and whipped cream (a little fruit, lots of cream) and eat it locked in the lavatory. I return to the table and sneak to the kitchen innumerable times for quiche. Quiche is healthy isn't it?

I return home alone and lonely. Watch telly and wait for Jason to call. He doesn't but my sister popped round. Right, tomorrow the diet will start, better stock up today. I whiz to the grocers – biscuits, fresh doughnuts and a quick stop at Burger King. Sugar for my sister, savoury for me. I pretend I've got a hungry boyfriend to the man at Burger King – I wish I had. Three large burgers, a chicken burger and some chips. I stuff it in my handbag and rush out. God I'm scared of being caught or even seen. I make it back to the safety of my home. My sister isn't hungry so I eat her food as well as mine. Shame to waste it. I never throw food away.

I smoke a joint and hope that it will dissolve the sick sense of disgust I have for myself. I want oblivion, I want to forget how much I ate today. I want out.

1994

I never thought I would not be starving or bingeing. Life was food. Today life is life. Some days are good, some are bad – but I love it. I am learning slowly to feel all five of my senses and to nourish myself emotionally and spiritually. What a journey recovery is. It's the getting there that counts, not just the destination. Sometimes I stumble, I graze my knee and it bleeds, but today I know how to get up, dust myself down and continue walking.

I am enjoying being in my own skin. I am learning to enjoy being me warts and all. The future is bright because today is bright. I let people in and myself out. I am learning to love. People bring joy to me that food never did. I know today that I cannot stick myself together with food, so I allow myself to be made whole by giving, receiving, laughing, crying, hoping and trusting. **9**

Elspeth

6 My first waking thought is of my weight. Did the amount that I ate the night before make me put on any weight? I panic, wondering how I'm going to face the day if I'm even 100g heavier than yesterday. It will be fine if I've lost weight but to have put any on will be a complete disaster.

I get out of bed, trying to be spritely and ready for another day at college, but my legs ache as I walk to the bathroom. I don't care about this as it makes me feel wonderful. It must mean that my muscles are now wasting which is why I find it difficult to walk. I firstly go to the loo to make sure that every drop of fluid is out of my body before I weigh myself. I then take all my clothes off, and every article of jewellery or accessory that I may be wearing, because otherwise it might add to my body weight. I get on the scales, half in fear of having gained but secretly knowing that I couldn't possibly have done so. To my relief the scales read 300g lighter than the day before. I'm ecstatic and my anorexia is telling me how much in control I am. I also think that it may mean I will allow myself to have a teaspoon full of ice-cream later on tonight.

Feeling relieved, I have a shower, always looking at my body and checking that all my bones are still sticking out in the right places. I then go and get dressed, making sure I'm wearing clothes that cleverly disguise my noticeably tumbling weight from all my friends at college.

When I'm dressed I go downstairs. I know I have to pretend I've had some breakfast just to keep my mother happy so I go to the kitchen and put a piece of toast in the toaster and switch on the kettle. I make toast and coffee and take them straight upstairs again, telling my mum that I'm in a hurry and that I've got to get my books ready for college. Once upstairs I take the toast from the plate and shove it quickly in a bag and put it at the bottom of my school bag so that I can get rid of it later. I then throw my coffee down the sink as I will not let a drop past my lips. I then run downstairs and leap in the car, trying to look as eager as possible at the thought of another tiring day at college. This is difficult as I feel constantly knackered, but I have to keep up the pretence for my mother.

Once I get to college I bury myself in my work, trying to squash my terrible hunger pangs that are constantly coming at me from my stomach. My mind races as I try to concentrate on an important English essay as well as dream about food. My mind dreams of allowing myself chocolate bars and packets of crisps, and I think of the meal that I would ideally like to eat there and then if I allowed myself. I torture myself and I know that if I wanted to I could eat these things like any other human being, but there is always the possibility that I will get fat and that is too big a risk to take.

At break times I rush to the recreation room to spend as much time as I can watching other people tucking into chocolate and sandwiches and crisps. Although I am starving, and it is torture for me, it feels wonderful because I feel in control and empty, and everyone else seems so weak because they let themselves eat. I often persuade my friends to eat more and love counting the amount of calories and realise how much more they are eating than me. This continues throughout the day – I am preoccupied with food throughout my lessons and watch with delight while everyone eats at break times.

I don't integrate to a great extent. I have a few friends but because I find my energy levels so low I can't laugh and joke around with fellow students. It takes all my energy just thinking and worrying about food.

When I get home in the evening I lie to my mother about the amount of food I have eaten during the day, claiming that I have had a massive lunch so I don't need to eat the meal that she has prepared that evening and that I will make something for myself later. As soon as I get home I go upstairs and stay in my room, really completely knackered, but burying myself in my work so as to take my mind off my hunger.

By the evening I am counting down the hours until 2 a.m. when I will allow myself to eat a miniscule amount, but to me this is the highlight of my day.

Often, when I know my parents are about to eat I go down to the kitchen to see what they are eating and count up all their calories. I feel great if they are having high-calorie foods and I often persuade my mum to use more cheese, or I mash the potato for her, putting loads of butter and milk in it.

I then make a quick exit as my mum is dishing out the food so as to escape possible confrontations.

Counting down the hours until 2 a.m., I try to keep myself busy watching TV, working, playing cards, etc. – but always on my own in my room. Occasionally I go down and talk to my mum if she asks me to but never for very long.

The minutes drag by as I become more and more hungry. I frequently look in my long mirror, just to check and reassure myself that my stomach has not grown and that my bones are still sticking out.

By late evening I am a mess. I am dying for 2 a.m. and very irritable. I haven't let a drop of food or drink pass my lips all day. I begin to plan what I might allow myself that evening – maybe a bit of cereal and I could possibly pick at the fruit or salad or cold vegetables left from my parents' supper.

The thing that I look forward to is a minute square of chocolate that I allow myself each night. At about 1 a.m. I run myself a bath and sit in there for about forty minutes to relax myself before my food. After that I make everything ready for bed and make sure my bedroom is spotlessly tidy.

At 2 a.m. on the dot I creep downstairs, hoping not to wake anyone. Firstly, when I arrive in the larder I pour myself a large glass of iced water as I am so thirsty. I then take the low-calorie cereal packets from the cupboard and begin to munch. It does not worry me so much and I often eat quite a lot of cereal (high fibre) and vegetables as I know they are low in calories and they will also keep my bowels moving so I will be able to feel empty after going to the loo.

Each night I allow myself half an hour maximum in the kitchen and not a minute over that. If I go over I panic dreadfully that I am losing control. As a special treat, if I feel I deserve it, I allow myself a couple of teaspoons of ice-cream, or maybe a pick at some cake or custard in the fridge, but I always keep it very regimented. I pour myself several glasses of water and drink it down quickly, half through a great thirst and half to bloat myself and therefore suppress any hunger.

I then make my way quietly upstairs again. On the way I take the one square of chocolate I allowed myself from our chocolate drawer. Once upstairs I get into bed and wait about an hour. By this time I am knackered but still I have to show myself that I have control by waiting before I eat the chocolate.

Eventually I get up and go to the loo to empty as much as I can before going to bed. I then creep back and allow myself my square of chocolate. I make it last for about half an hour, savouring every crumb, as I know that this is the last I will have for another twenty-four hours.

Finally, I allow myself to sleep at about 4 a.m. I hardly sleep at all, feeling uncomfortable but knackered. I only leave myself about 3-4 hours of sleep before I have to be up again for college the next morning.

13

Take the try out and do

Stop making excuses to yourself

If there is one word that I hear more in my working day than any other, it is the word *try*. The majority of clients who come to see me have all been trying to do different things to help themselves with their addictions. The alcoholic is trying not to drink – the drug addict is trying not to take drugs – the exercise fanatic is trying to cut down – the compulsive gambler is trying to stop gambling. The person with an eating disorder is trying not to eat certain foods, trying to stay on a diet, trying to take exercise, trying not to walk past certain food shops, trying not to open the fridge, trying not to look at other people's food, trying not to compare themselves with other people, trying to count calories, trying not to let other people know, trying to hide food, trying to hide the shame, loneliness and that overriding sense of failure that you feel because you can't seem to do anything other than *try*.

Have you ever thought that every time you try and fail, it feels as though you are breaking a promise to yourself. I know that you don't mean to fail. I know how much you promised yourself that this would be the last binge, or the last time you'd take laxatives, or starve yourself. I know that when you said it, you meant it, but look what happens the minute you get into food – the promises go out of the window. Please don't get me wrong, I'm not judging you or saying you're a bad person or that you're useless and can't keep a promise I am just driving the point home to you that you are powerless over this – you've got an addiction, so you can't do anything else other than what you're doing. 'Here he goes again,' you might say, 'telling me all the things that I haven't been doing'. Does this sound as though I'm preaching to you? Do I sound like a schoolmaster, or a concerned parent? Well, I don't really care if I sound like all of these put together, that's fine with me, if it will only help you realize what you are doing to yourself and what is happening to you. It's time to stop all this trying and start to do.

We are nearly at the end of this book and it's getting time to make some decisions, if you haven't made them already. There is no future in what you are doing to yourself. Only the torment and unhappiness that it's bringing you at the moment. Every time you go to the fridge or the cupboard, what you are actually doing is giving all your power away, you are giving your total self-control to your addiction. Now if there was anything positive in this or if there were any gain or healthy result, I would be the first one to tell you to keep doing it because it's good for you – but it's not good for you – and there is nothing positive about what you are doing.

Imagine the scenario: you've bought a jumper or a coat, or a pair of trousers from a large store. You hadn't tried it on when you'd bought it, and when you get home you find that it's the wrong size. So you return to the store and go to the refund counter where you can either exchange your item of clothing or get a refund. Now imagine the same situation happening when you go to your fridge, cupboard, supermarket or sweet shop. All you're getting when you buy the foods that you shouldn't be eating is misery. It's like a big misery refund. You do not get any happiness from it. You may think that you do, but it is very short lived. All you get are those feelings of disgust and self-loathing, and on it goes. You keep saying, 'Well, I'm trying to do something about this.' You're probably thinking now, 'Beechy, I've been trying for years!' I agree, you've been *trying* for years, but you haven't been *doing*.

So you must start doing now. The trying stops right now. Let me help you a little bit. Why don't you make a list of all the things that you've been trying to do. A list as long as you can make it of all the different activities, promises, commitments or whatever it is that you've been trying to do. Have a look at it and be very honest with this question: 'What has got in the way of you doing any of these things?' I guarantee that it would have been because of your eating. Your addiction has got in the way, and you are powerless over the food which is getting in the way of your life.

Now I know I've been going on and on throughout this book about how powerless and unmanageable you are, but I have to do this, you must understand this because I have to get this point home to you. You need to accept your powerlessness and unmanageability because at this point you will start to do rather than try. I know that you can probably give me many excuses why things haven't worked, how hard you've tried and how difficult things are for you. I know all this, but I also know that because of your eating disorder you have changed from the person you used to be.

Progression of symptoms

Compulsive overeating

Food alters the way you feel, it alters the way you behave, it changes your moods, and leads you into that false sense of security; by that I mean when you have that occasional binge and you think that it will relieve your anxiety, when really what you are worried about is your low self-esteem. Then you'll find that you are eating when you are not hungry, and after you've overeaten you'll feel guilty, and have feelings of remorse. You will have tried various diets, and you'll fall into the trap of feeling that all your self-worth depends on how much weight you can lose. Then, when you lose the weight, the weight loss is only temporary. You fall back into your old ways and regain the weight. Sometimes more than you had before. Then you worry and you skip meals, you feel so hungry that you start to binge at night, and you develop poor impulse control, you have a constant concern with your weight and body image. Then the mood swings start, and you will increase your dependency on your over or undereating. You will have enormous feelings of embarrassment, and underneath this you'll have this fear of your bingeing and of how out of control your eating is getting. This, in turn, increases your anxiety level and alienates you even more from people, because how can you tell them what is going on with you? This can force you to become very depressed and more isolated. You find it increasingly difficult to discuss your problems and in the middle of all this you keep trying and trying to do something about it.

Can you start to get the picture and see what is happening? Look at the way your life is being affected here. Look at the way other people are affected. Your friends and family will notice changes in you, your work will be affected and you will be isolated socially. You will distance yourself totally from people. That is why I am asking you to start doing something now before this gets worse. Yes, it gets worse. Don't think that it's just going to stay like this because it's not. I've taken you through the early stage symptoms to the middle-stage symptoms. It will then go on to be crucial. You will start to suffer persistent remorse, your binges will increase. You'll feel hopeless. You'll start to tell more lies, and have unreasonable resentments. You will have a fear of going out. Your weight is going to affect the way you live you life. Your general health will suffer and you'll have constant physical problems. By this stage you may move on and try alcohol or drugs to help you with your problem. This isn't a tale of someone else – it is what will happen to you if you don't start doing something about all this. It is too late in the day to carry on with it. The total recognition that you need help needs to start now.

Anorexia

For those of you suffering from anorexia, the same applies, your illness starts off with low self-esteem, you move to the misperception of hunger and feelings of lack of control in your life. Then comes a distorted body image, your over-achieving takes over to try to compensate all those feelings of low self-worth. Your anxiety increases. Starving causes your menstrual cycle to stop. You isolate yourself from family and friends. Your perfectionist behaviour increases. You may get into compulsive exercising and you will almost certainly eat alone. You will be fighting with your family because they won't know what to do. They will be watching someone that they love starving themselves before their very eyes. They will be blaming themselves, they'll go to any lengths to help you, and what they will be met with is someone who is totally numbed from any normal feelings. Imagine how your family will feel? On the physical side you will have increased facial and body hair. You will have decreased scalp hair and you will start to display an emaciated appearance.

This is starting to get crucial – this is dangerous – you will be very depressed and your fear of food will increase because you will be so paranoid about gaining weight. You will now be in a state of malnutrition. You will have tyrannical mood swings. You won't be able to think rationally. You will not be able to make decisions, and again the people around you, most predominantly your family, will be suffering the conse-quences along with you. Your physical problems are going to increase, you'll have electrolyte imbalance, feel very weak, and develop dental problems. You will have difficulty walking and sitting, and you'll have total sleep disturbance. I could go on and on. These are things that you have to be very aware of. You are entering into something that is totally life threat-ening.

Bulimia

Again we start with low self-esteem, and the feelings that your self-worth is based upon a low weight. You will become very dependent on other people for approval. Again you will have a distorted image of your normal weight. You may start to experiment with vomiting, using laxatives or diuretics, you will very quickly get out of control. There will be a high element of embarrassment, anxiety and depression because of this behaviour. You will start to eat alone, and you will become totally preoccupied with eating and food. Your fear of bingeing will increase and you'll very quickly realise how out of control you are becoming. By inducing vomiting, using laxatives or diuretics, you are inviting gastro-intestinal problems. By constantly vomiting you will get tooth damage, gum disease, chronic sore throats, difficulty breathing and swallowing. You will also suffer from hypoglycaemia, abnormally low potassium levels and electrolyte imbalance. Your health will deteriorate and you'll have constant physical problems. You run a high possibility of rupturing your heart. You will suffer from dehydration and irregular heart rhythms. You may fall into a depression where you will contemplate suicide. This is crucial – it is very serious.

Please look back over what I have just written for you. I have given you a very clear picture of a person who is overeating, a person who is suffering from anorexia nervosa, and a person who is suffering from bulimia.

These are the things that happen in the early, middle and crucial stages. This is the road that you will walk if you are not already walking it. What I am imploring you to do is accept some help, get off this road to destruction, and get on the road to recovery. Recovery is possible, but the first thing that you've got to do is accept what is happening to you.

Ask for some help, accept that you are out of control and that what you are doing to yourself is not an answer to your problems. Food is not going to solve anything. I am very clearly saying to you that your problems lie in your feelings, not in the abuse of food. You can argue all you want with me, but I think that by looking at your own consequences, honestly and rationally, you will very quickly see what is happening to you.

At this very moment, you can make a decision that this is going to stop, and for the first time you are going to take the try out and do something about this to secure yourself the first step on the road to recovery. It's not going to be easy, but I'm with you every step of the way. You can get through this. You can recover and have some happiness in your life at last.

How to help yourself

Compulsive overeating

1. As I have said before you *need* to stick to three meals and avoid snacks. It is also so important to avoid 'trigger foods'.

2. When you are going to have a meal – SIT DOWN. Don't eat rushing around. Why not lay the table (even if it is in the kitchen) and let yourself start to enjoy your food by eating SLOWLY.

3. Don't confuse hunger with thirst. If you think you are hungry in between meals, STOP. Have a drink of tea, coffee, mineral water, etc. and just wait.

4. KEEP BUSY. DON'T sit and think and obsess. DO SOMETHING OR RING SOMEBODY.

5. Work on you feelings diary. Are you hungry? Or are you FEELING? Don't confuse a feeling with being HUNGRY.

6. Don't keep going to the fridge/food cupboard or shops. Why torture yourself? Go when it is *necessary* and consider whether it is wise to buy in bulk.

Bulimics (who purge)

See above 1, 2, 3, 4, 5, 6.

7. You may not be used to 'feeling full'. Learn to accept that keeping food down will NOT make you fat if you haven't overeaten. Keep telling yourself this. Reassure yourself and AFFIRM YOURSELF.

8. Avoid going to the bathroom straight after you have

eaten. If you need to, ring somebody or sit and write.

9.   If you have been drinking a lot of fluid to help you purge, STOP – it is OLD BEHAVIOUR! Drinking fluid is healthy, but it doesn't have to be excessive.

Anorexics

See above: 1, 2, 3, 4, 5, 6.

10.   When I say 'Keep busy' I don't mean rush around. I also know that there is a part of you dying to eat. You *must* sit down to eat and stay there for a while. Keep telling yourself that you are worth it. Again AFFIRM yourself.

11.   Avoid filling up with water (whether you purge or not).

12.   Stay away from tight belts and waistbands. If you eat you will feel fuller – THAT IS NORMAL! Don't constrict yourself or try and measure.

14

The last hurdle

But don't expect miracles overnight

Throughout the book we've looked extensively at your behaviour around food. I know it hasn't been easy to read, but I also know that it's not easy to live with and, if you don't do something about your problem it's not going to go – it's going to get worse. So the last hurdle is really a question of you making up your mind what you want to do about your eating disorder.

Do you want things to stay the way they are? If so, that's fine. If you can live with all this, then go ahead, keep doing it, there is nothing I or anybody else can do if that is your decision. I find it extremely hard to say this because every day I see the consequences of people overeating, undereating, inducing vomiting, taking laxatives or just generally abusing themselves with food, and I watch what happens to the person emotionally. I watch them destroy themselves and take away the only self-worth that they've ever had, bit by bit. So if you think that I am sanctimoniously sitting writing this book and just dishing it out to you, you're wrong. I'm very much involved in this.

As I said earlier on, there's a war on – it's called the Weight War. Wherever you look women, men, teenagers and people of every age are trying to lose weight, gain weight or control their weight, and I know that this is something that is not going to change or go away overnight, but at least what I've been able to do in this book is to be honest with you and maybe, I hope, it will help you confront your fears, come through the pain of the past and help you realize that you are a good person, that you do deserve more than this, that you have a right to recover and that there are good things that can happen in your life. You have a lot of unused potential which you just haven't been able to get at because you've been so preoccupied with food. So here's your chance – here is your chance to change all this.

At the start of this book you were given the chance to define what constitutes an eating disorder, and for you to make a decision, through a very easy questionnaire, whether you have an eating disorder or not. Most probably you've known that you've had an eating disorder long before you picked up this book. Nevertheless, it's very important for you to get a clear picture of what you see as a problem, because you're the one who has a war with food, and deep inside you have all the answers – you hold the key for your recovery.

In different parts of this book we've talked about the eating disorder that overeats, the eating disorder that under-eats, and the eating disorder that takes diuretics, laxatives or induces vomiting. But really what we are talking about is people. You are a person, an individual and unless you've got a twin that looks exactly like you, you are unique. There is no one that smiles like you or laughs like you or who has an identical sense of humour. You see this is what makes you a unique individual and with that you have individual needs. It is important while you're reading this book that you focus on you – not on other people and not on your family – but you because it's you who will be making the changes and doing all the hard work, so it is important for you to stay centred, and to remember as we talked about earlier, 'It's your feelings not the food'.

Food is the medicator for your unhappiness, for your low self-worth, for those insecure feelings and feelings of loneliness. So where do we go from here? How do we get over this last hurdle, stay over it and make it a hurdle of the past? Something that is just a memory and not a constant reality? How do we do this? Well, believe it or not, by getting this far in the book you've already started. If you think about and look back at what you've covered through the chapters you will see that you've got a clear road – it depends on whether you want to walk it or not.

Key points

Let's go back for a few minutes. Can you remember that in Chapter 2 I explained to you that compulsive overeating, bulimia, anorexia and binge eating are illnesses, they are conditions, they are not normal things to do? I was asking you to let yourself off the hook as you weren't supposed to know that you had an illness or a medical condition – how would you? Unless, I said, I'm sure you would have done something by now if you had known.

Thinking about feelings

I gave you an assignment in Chapter 2 which was to look at the list of feelings that I'd written, and for you to start to think about your feelings – become more aware of them, and start to identify how they affect you. Go back and have a look at that list, can you see the changes you've made? Can you see how much clearer you are and how quickly you can identify the way you are feeling? Don't discount this progress you have made because it is really important to look at how far you've come. You see one of the things that you don't do, or haven't done in the past, is to start to give yourself affirmation. You will start to give yourself plenty of negatives and tell yourself how useless and worthless you are, but you won't have been telling yourself that you're worthwhile, that you can make some changes and that you can get better.

Living in the present

Have you become a human doing rather than a human being? Has your life become dominated with food? Either avoiding it, eating it, or thinking about it. We discussed how you lose your values, how your self-worth plummets, how you are manipulated by food, how your happiness is determined by food and how, at the end of the day, food totally takes over your life and you end up on the treadmill towards disaster without seeing any way to get off it. That's why it is so important that you live in today and not in tomorrow or next week.

You must look to today, not the future. If you think about it the future is based on what you do today. Think back for a moment about one of the diets you've been on and how you told yourself that this was going to be the one, and how you promised yourself that you were going to lose weight and stick to it and become thin; your future was going to be so different when you stopped carrying this weight around with you. What happened? You gave yourself such high expectations, that before you knew it you were back to bingeing again – caught in the same old trap.

The same applies if you've been suffering from anorexia. You tell yourself that you are going to put on weight, that you're going to start eating, and not be so controlled by food, and that in six months time you are going to have gained X amount of weight, but look what happens. You attempt to eat double or treble the amount of what you normally have and before you know it you are engrossed in fear, you become totally terrified – why? Well, just look at the expectations – look what you're asking of yourself. Can you really expect to go from eating practically nothing to eating three large meals a day? It isn't possible, you have to very gently reintroduce food into your life.

Learning to look after yourself

Go back and have a look at Chapter 5. In this chapter you will see that I talk about learning to be good to yourself on six different levels: emotionally, physically, mentally, socially, spiritually and also taking responsibility for yourself. You must accept the enormity of what has been happening to you and how unrealistic it is for you to think that you can change this pattern of destructive behaviour overnight. It is going to take time and a lot of courage and strength. One of the ways that you can give yourself courage and strength is by learning to affirm yourself. Now, I know this is really difficult. The hardest thing in the world to do when you don't feel good about yourself is to start to tell yourself that you're OK, that you're a good person, that you're worth something, that you can succeed and recover and that you are worth recovering for. I know it is hard, but you have to make a start at it.

Self-affirmation

Look at Chapter 6, I asked you to write a list of what you liked about yourself as an individual. Now I can imagine that this was difficult as I was asking you to take a look at yourself – you, not anyone else – because it isn't what other people think that's important. That is what you've been living on. You've been trying to get gratification and the approval of everyone else around you. But it's what you think about yourself that is ultimately important. It is you who you're getting well for – not other people.

I also asked you in Chapter 6 to have a look at how you approach life, and how important it is for you to see yourself, not as a loser, but as someone who can be a winner – someone who can do something other than be obsessed with food. Just to be able to tell yourself that you are doing the best you can and that you are worth doing it for will help you on a daily basis to start to learn to affirm yourself. At this stage self-affirmation is going to be so important in getting you over the last hurdle towards recovery. So remember what I said in Chapter 6 – take some time to yourself – take stock of your day and remember you are worth it.

You have a right to recover and a right to feel good about yourself. At this stage it is really important for you to allow yourself to get excited about what is going to happen. Just think how long you've been negative and how long you've been writing yourself off . . . or all the times you wished that you were able to do something about your eating. Think about those times when you've been walking past shop windows and you've looked at the clothes and thought, 'I wish I could get into that dress, or suit.' Or the times you've been on holiday and wished you could get into a bathing costume without feeling so self-conscious, or walk around in a bathing costume without having to wear a towel over your bottom because you feel so big. It is time for some of those wishes to come true, and the way they are going to come true is by you changing your habits.

Self-assessment

If you look at Chapter 7, I talked about the necessity and the importance of changing your habits around your behaviour with food. Remember the expression, 'Keep doing what you're doing and you'll keep getting what you've got.' In that chapter I asked you to write out a self-assessment to get a picture of the way your eating disorder had affected your life. Have another look at that self-assessment. Look at how powerless and unmanageable you've become with food, and consequently with your behaviour. Look at the way everyone around you has been affected. You can't give me any more excuses. Look what you've written. Look at your own truth. Look at what's been happening to you. The picture is very clear to see. Your whole life is affected by your eating and consequently your family and friends are affected. You really can't delude yourself any longer. The truth is before you in black and white, and it is time to make some changes, and you can if you want to.

It is so important for you to believe that this time you can. This time you can succeed without falling into the old traps like you have before, because the difference this time is that it's not a diet. We're not talking about you starving yourself, or if you're undereating, we're not talking about suddenly increasing your intake of food. I am asking you to look at your problems in a totally different way. I am asking you to explore your feelings about yourself and to look at your self-esteem and begin to understand the impact food has had on your life.

I asked you in Chapter 6 to keep a diary to help you understand your relationship with food and to get a clear understanding of how much it affects your life – because that's really what this book is about. It's about you having a life that isn't dominated by food. It's about you being able to sit down at a table, eat and get up feeling satisfied with what you've eaten, rather than wanting to eat more and more. It's about you getting up from the table and not going to the bathroom to induce vomiting, or taking twenty or thirty laxatives before you sit down. It's about you being able to eat with your family, rather than sitting alone eating and feeling isolated and withdrawn.

This book is about you eating to live rather than living to eat. For those of you who have been suffering from anorexia it's time to come off the hunger strike, as we discussed in Chapter 8. It's time to let go of all that control – not only around food but around people, because you know how much power you have. Don't tell me that you haven't noticed the effect you have on your family or friends or how concerned they continually are because of your behaviour around food or because of the level of your weight. This behaviour is only going to lead you into a life-threatening condition, one which you may not recover from.

Have a look at your 'Day in the life' that I asked you to write in Chapter 12. Look at what has been happening to you, and as you read your 'Day in the life' you may feel as if you are reading about somebody else – but you're not – you're reading about you. Can you see what's happening? Can you understand how important it is for you to do something about this behaviour before it gets too serious? Can you see that you are *dying* to be thin? I know how frightening it is to face all this. It's terrifying. I am not for one minute underestimating how difficult it is, but I have to say it to you straight out like this because if I don't, what will happen? You are just going to keep doing the same thing until it is too late and physically your body won't be able to take any more, and the inevitable will happen.

Facing your fear

I am asking you to face your fear, as I talked about in Chapter 3. If you don't face your fears you will stay exactly where you are. Have a look in the mirror – you may think that you're overweight, but really what you are looking at is a shadow of yourself, a shadow of what you used to be: there is no vibrance, there is no life in your eyes, there is no colour in your skin and there is no enthusiasm. Look what has happened. Look what you have become. Is this the way you want it to stay? Is this the way that you want to be? If that's the case there is really nothing I can do or say. I could write ten books, but if you're not willing to take the advice, stand up for yourself and ask for some help, then no one can help you. So ask for help, put down that self-defeating pride, you can't do this on your own. You've tried and look what has happened. You need support and you need to be shown the way. Your way isn't working for you. You need to start listening to other people who know what they are talking about and who have the knowledge and expertise to help you get through this.

Another danger is that you could be one of those people who I talked about in Chapter 9 who has managed to hide their eating disorder. Even though you've got the perfect figure, inside you are crying out for help because the price you are paying to keep your perfect figure is so high. So, again, the need to ask for help and to take professional advice is imperative.

The bottom line is that you're trapped, trapped in the fridge. Whether you are a compulsive overeater, a bulimic or an anorexic, you are all trapped in the fridge. What I mean by that is that you are obsessed by food. Whether it's eating it or not, it's the same thing. Most of your waking day is taken up by thinking about food. Have a look at the collage that I asked you to do in Chapter 5. Have a look at how you are trapped in the fridge. Look what the food and the obsession with it is doing to you. I am running through the chapters that I have written because it is important for you to get the full picture of what is happening so that we can get all our strength together to get over this last hurdle and to start your road to a full recovery.

If you need more identification, look back at Chapter 12 and you will get all the identification you need. If you look through the various 'Days in the Lives' of the people who have been kind enough to share their day with you, you will see the similarities rather than the differences. You will find yourself in each one of those days. Again this should give you a clear indication of what is happening to you.

The circumstances may be different but the consequences will be the same because at the end of every one of those 'Days in the Lives' is that unending feeling of despair and loneliness that comes from thinking that you are the only one who suffers from this. How can you tell anybody else how you're feeling because they won't understand? But if you look at Chapter 3 you will see that you are not the only one. There are countless people who are feeling like you do and there are countless people getting well, simply because they are asking for help, using the support system offered to them and listening to the advice they've been given. They are not arguing, they are actually accepting the help and taking responsibility, and for the first time in their lives taking a good look around them and getting a picture of how much damage has been done to them and to the people around them, such as their family.

In Chapter 11 we saw very clearly that this is a family affair. You may do all the overeating, undereating, purging or bingeing on your own but your behaviour will spill over onto other people. The people that will suffer most are your family. Have a look back at Chapter 11 and look at the rules that the family construct to try to cope with your behaviour. I know that this is difficult for you to read the first time around, but please go back and have another look because the more you see what has been happening, the more likely you are to take these last few steps and get over this last hurdle.

As I wrote in Chapter 6, you are worth more than this. You were not born to destroy yourself and continually to punish yourself. You have a right to some happiness and for some real feelings of self-worth. You can come right back at me and say, 'Oh Beechy, I've been trying to get these feelings, I've been doing everything I can.' But have you? You see you always seem to use the word 'try' and, as I said in Chapter 13, you've got to take the try out and do. You've got to start doing things. Trying doesn't achieve anything it's the doing that wins and you've got to start becoming a winner and start believing that you can recover and that you are going to start now.

You are going to need all the self-belief that you can muster and all the support that you can gather together to jump this last hurdle, move into the action phase of your recovery and start to enjoy the benefits of getting well. Imagine what it would be like actually to feel good about yourself – to stand in front of the mirror and say, 'You really are OK, you really are worth something.' Can you imagine for one moment what that would feel like? As you are reading this you are probably thinking, 'I'll never be able to do that or feel like that. Well, I'm telling you that if you are willing to put the work in, take responsibility, be honest with yourself and jump over this last hurdle, you can recover and have the good things that you deserve in life and hopefully become the person that you want to be rather than who your eating disorder has created. So it's decision time. Are you going to make this jump over this last hurdle or are you going to stay where you are: The choice is yours – I'm ready if you are.

15
Steps to freedom

Understanding, accepting and asking for help

First of all let me congratulate you on getting this far with the book. I know that it hasn't been easy and I realize that I've asked you to look at yourself in a way that you haven't done before. I hope that it has helped you get a picture of what needs to change for you. In a way I feel sad that this is the last chapter in the book because I feel as though I've been on a journey with you, a journey that I hope you will continue, and I've no doubt that if you do, you will get all the benefits that recovery brings.

You will also have something in your life that you've never had before which is, quite simply, choice. The only choices around food you've had are to either overeat, starve yourself or purge and induce vomiting – you haven't had any healthy choices. Imagine what it is going to feel like not having to overeat. The choice to be a better person; the choice to care for yourself and the people around you; the choice to tell others how you've been able to overcome your eating disorder, so that they'll be able to help themselves. The choices are endless and all you have to do is take some steps to freedom.

The first step has got to be *acceptance* – acceptance that you have a problem, that your eating disorder is out of control and that you can't control it – acceptance that you are going to need some help as you can't do this on your own. You may need medical attention or the help of a therapist or a self-help group or possibly at a rehabilitation centre (in-patient or out-patient). You must accept that you need the help. This is the first step towards your freedom.

Actually *asking for help* has got to be the second step, because without you asking nothing is going to happen. Your wife, husband or children can try to get you to do something but if you don't actually ask, nothing is going to change.

This is a very difficult step to take because, again, it's about giving up the control. It's about you saying, 'I can't do this on my own.' It's about you admitting that you have a problem. It's about you sitting down maybe with your wife/husband or the whole family or friends and saying, 'Yes, you were right, I was telling lies, but I couldn't tell you as I felt so shameful.' It's about you getting really honest and this is so difficult because you've been living a lie for so long. Think back on the times when you've had to lie about your food intake or what happened to food that you weren't supposed to eat, or someone finding sweet papers and candy bars that you'd hidden and you'd forgotten about. Can you remember what that was like? Those feelings of shame at being caught out. But, even then, that didn't stop you telling a lie to try to cover it up did it? You had to, you couldn't do anything else but tell lies as you weren't responsible for what you were doing. Remember that your eating disorder is a condition – it's a compulsive behaviour and once you are in that behaviour you can't do anything else other than what you are doing.

Understanding that you suffer from a condition rather than continually blaming yourself for being a bad and dishonest person is really going to help you to ask for help. You weren't responsible when you were using food and bingeing, but you are responsible today, and it's today that matters. It's today that you can make the choice – it's today that you can lift the telephone or go and see your doctor or see a professional who knows about eating disorders. It's today that you can change your life and break free from the obsession and compulsion that's been driving you to destroy yourself. Today's decision is tomorrow's freedom. Freedom from all the loneliness and darkness – freedom to see some light, to have some future, to have success no matter what you do, who you are or where you come from.

You deserve the chance to live and to make the best possible future for yourself, and for your family to get some happiness and get back the person who they love. You can do this. You are worth this. You deserve this, and just by living one day at a time with no days off. What I mean by no days off is having continuity and sticking to your eating plan – not just doing it for four days and then eating what you want. I'm talking about seven days a week and it's not rigid, it's not a sentence – it's just a way of living, it's a way of you living instead of dying inside. That's what you've been doing, letting the food take the whole control of your life and you've seen or felt nothing except the misery that your behaviour brings. So I'm talking about a day at a time of looking after yourself, being good to yourself and if you do that you will get all the healthy results that you deserve.

The next step is *commitment*, and what I mean by this is that you must make up your mind that this is what you need and want to do. Think of all the times when you went on a diet or changed your eating habits, or started to eat, or stopped taking laxatives, or cut down your vomiting, because other people had been nagging at you or repeatedly telling you that you should do this. So, angrily, or reluctantly you went on a diet, or started to eat a little bit more, or stopped taking so many laxatives, etc. but, deep inside, you didn't want to because you were still stuck in the denial of your illness, or maybe it was just the plain fact that you weren't ready or because you were so frightened. Whatever the reasons, if you think back, you will come up with the same conclusions that it didn't work because *you* didn't make the decision, other people made it for you.

So what I mean by commitment is *your* commitment – your promise to yourself that today you are going to do it for you. You're going to put all the past times and all the past failures out of your mind and today is going to be different. Using the support system around you will be a vital step in your getting well. I know that you want to show everybody because in

the past you've felt a failure, and I know you want everyone
to sit up and take notice of what you are doing. At this point
I have to say to you to be careful about this because people
won't know that it is going to be any different, how would
they? They've seen it all before, they've heard about all the
wonder diets, slimming drinks and slimming tablets. They've
heard, 'This is the last binge,' 'This is the last laxative,' or
'I'm going to start eating and gain some weight,' 'I'm going
to start looking after myself'. They've heard it all before. But
what's really going to make the difference this time is continuity, commitment and the acceptance that it's not going to
happen overnight. Remember that you are not doing this for
anyone else but for you. I know you want everyone to take
notice, because you feel that if they do this you will get an
extra spur to really go for it, but what I'm saying is don't
expect this to happen. If it does then it's a bonus, but if it
doesn't, just hang in there because it will come in time,
people will notice, but they'll only really start taking you seriously when *you* start taking *this* seriously. So use the support.

The first thing is to use your doctor to check you out and
see that everything is OK medically because you don't know
what's been happening. Even if you feel that there is nothing
wrong and that it's silly and time wasting – go anyway. Don't
play around with your body. Use self-help groups and, as I've
said earlier on in the book, there is a lot of help available.
There are many different self-help groups, you can find one
which will suit you. Check them out and check out the commitment within those groups. Check out the people who
really want to get well because those are the people who you
should stick with. You've got to stick with the winners. You've
got to stick with the people who really want to break free
from the chains of this illness.

Find yourself a therapist or a counsellor. This is really
important because you do need someone to talk to.
Someone who you can trust and who isn't going to go and
tell everybody else what you've said, somewhere where you
can go and dump all those feelings that you don't need to
carry around with you, and to get some feedback from your

therapist or counsellor. You can very quickly say to me that you've got plenty of friends who you can talk to – plenty of good friends who have been there for you and who will listen to you. I understand that and I'm not saying that they are not good friends. What I'm saying is that they haven't got the professional expertise and training to help you through some of the emotional traumas that you've been going through. The other thing about friends is that they tell you what you want to hear. A good therapist will not do that. He or she will tell you what you need to hear and there is a difference between these. He or she will be able to differentiate between your wants and your needs. Your wants aren't important but your needs are. So get in some medical input using the self-help available. Get yourself some sessions with a counsellor or a therapist. Seeing a nutritionist can be very important because they can help you with a proper eating plan if you are having difficulty with that. Remember you've been eating very erratically and not like other people. You may not know what proper portions are. A food plan is very important in your recovery. It needs to become part of your living day because that's what we're talking about you doing. Living.

Starting to live again

Remember what that is? Having a future, having some fun, not being continually obsessed with food, getting into a healthy relationship, or turning your present relationship into something that is functional rather than dysfunctional, doing the things you want to do, rather than just dreaming about doing them, and having choices. That's what we are talking about – living – and using all the support available to you.

Exercise

The next step to take towards freedom is to devise yourself an *exercise plan.* Now you and I know that exercise hasn't been one of your greatest fortes, or maybe you'd like to call walking to the fridge, driving to the supermarket, or walking to your nearest food shop and back, exercise – but I don't really think that is what we are talking about. You need to get back in shape. Remember the bombardment that your body has been taking with food. You haven't been looking after yourself. So you need, very gently, to start with, to get back in shape. Again I will ask you to consult your doctor because, as I've said before, it is important that we go about things in the correct way. Consulting your doctor on your physical well-being is an all-important part of your recovery, and most certainly a must if you are going to undertake an exercise programme. So, doctor first.

Finding yourself somewhere to exercise may, at first glance, be difficult for you, because you may feel intimidated or embarrassed about going along to a fitness club or your local gym. Perhaps you don't want people to look at you as you feel embarrassed about your appearance, or maybe you think that everyone is fitter than you, or that they look better than you and exercise for longer. That's just marching straight back into your old behaviour isn't it? That's you telling yourself again that you are not going to be good at anything, and that everyone else is better than you. Remember you've got to start somewhere. I mean be realistic with yourself. How can you walk into a gymnasium for the first time and expect to be the fittest person there? How can you, when you've only just started to look after yourself and tell yourself that things are going to change in your life. You can't expect things to change within twenty-four hours. I know that you want what you want yesterday, but welcome to the real world, this is going to be a slow process.

So you've got to put down that *self-defeating pride,* again, and find yourself somewhere to exercise. Or it could be that you may want to do it in the privacy of your own home. You can start off by doing some gentle exercises for ten to fifteen minutes every day. You could also buy yourself some books on stretching exercises or a video that you can work out to.

Maybe this is what you could do before you go to the gym and perhaps this is a good way of helping you with your feelings of embarrassment or those feelings that you are not good enough and fear that everyone will laugh at you. Whatever way you do it, you've got to make a start and there are lots of different ways that you can do this.

An exercise plan is not only going to help you to get your body in shape, it will also help you to revitalise a lot of lost energy. Have you noticed how lethargic you've been feeling in the past few months or years? Have you noticed that you haven't got much energy around you? Well now we're going to get some and this energy is going to be very positive for you.

You are going to feel very different – you will look different — you will talk differently and you will think differently. Imagine all this – imagine the freedom you are going to feel? Yes, I'm talking about you, not someone else but *you*. You can attain all this if you will just start to take these steps.

Using your potential

The next step to take is using the *potential* that you have. Now don't give me that quizzical look as you're reading this, 'What potential is he talking about?' You might ask. I'm talking about all that unused potential that you've got, but you haven't been using any of it because all your energy has gone into abusing food. Ask yourself how much commitment you've really put into things that you've tried in the past. If you are really honest your answer will be, 'Not much, because I was more preoccupied in eating or my behaviour around food.' I'm talking about the unused potential you have for being a better parent, sister, brother, friend or colleague. Or the creative side of you that you haven't used for a long time, or maybe you've never even tried to use it. The list is endless. You've had the potential to go through this book with me and that hasn't been easy, that tells me how much potential you've got. First and foremost the potential to change. You may not feel as though you have much potential in you at the moment, but I am convinced that you have, so why not trust me on this one, let me believe you have the potential and let's go for it.

Taking your time

The next step towards freedom is *taking your time*. Yes, quite simply, taking you time. You always want to rush things. You want what you want when you want it, and you want it yesterday. But it doesn't work like that, you've got to slow down and take your time. This is for the rest of your life, a day at a time. So there is no need to rush, there's no need to compare yourself anymore, there's no need for you to strive to do better than anybody else, this is all for you, and all the benefits are for you. Now I know this sounds as if I'm asking you to be selfish, and you're right, I am. I am asking you to be more selfish than you've ever been and put you first.

I'm asking you to stand up and say, 'This one's for me – my recovery comes first,' because without your recovery what will happen to you? Just close your eyes for a moment and think back to your last binge, or your last purge or vomiting bout or your last spate of starving or taking laxatives, just think of the darkness, loneliness, deprivation, humiliation, alienation and the total despair you felt. Just think about that for a moment. Now don't try to run away in your thoughts – stay with those feelings. Are you getting a sense of how bad it was? Are you getting a picture of the nightmare? Do you feel yourself going cold at the thought of it? I hope so – I hope you'll never forget those feelings and how bad they were, because if you do, you'll go back there again.

You must not forget – but having said that you need not punish yourself, and I'm asking you to wake up out of that nightmare, not to run, just to take your time. There is no need to run because you are going to change yourself physically, mentally, emotionally, spiritually and sexually. You're looking at your whole person. It's not a diet anymore – it's OK, you don't need to be on the run. So just take your time, a day at a time, and everything will fall into place.

Boosting self-esteem

The next step is looking after your *self-worth*. I know that this is a really difficult step for you because it's been so long since you actually affirmed yourself, or even thought about doing anything like that. It's been hard enough for you to look in the mirror. It's been hard enough for you to even look at photographs of yourself but, like the rest of the steps towards freedom, I'm asking you to be brave and really break new ground for yourself. Coming out of your eating disorder is coming into yourself and you've got to start looking at yourself, and affirming yourself for who you really are rather than who you're not. If you find that hard to understand, just think about how much you've been negating yourself and telling yourself that you're not worth it or how disgusting you are. Well, I'm telling you today that you are somebody, that you're not disgusting, that you're worth every good thing that happens to you, and that you have a right to get better, and a right to make a new life for yourself – but you've got to play a big part in this.

You've really got to tell yourself all the positive things that you can. To start with things are going to be difficult, but just go gently and you can do it. Go back to the chapter I wrote on affirmations and that will help you with this. Remember that you are worth doing this for.

Having some fun

Your next step towards freedom is *enjoying your recovery*. Yes enjoy it. This is not supposed to be a miserable, sad, unhappy experience for you. I know it's difficult and painful and emotionally draining, but there has got to be some enjoyment in it. From the very moment that you decided to make a change, you should actually say to yourself that it was an enjoyable experience, because you are lifting yourself out of the darkness. Lots of enjoyable things will start happening to you. Remember you've spent the best part of your life being miserable and telling yourself that you'll never enjoy anything – whether it's because you don't want to or because you felt that you weren't worth it. Well it's time to start having some fun. Yes that three letter word *fun*. When is the last time you had some? Think for a moment. It's time for some happiness in your life. If your recovery is not going to have some fun and happiness in it, tell me what is the point? What is the point in you having done all this hard work on yourself if you're not going to have some enjoyment. So come on, let's get some.

Reclaiming your life

You last step towards freedom is *taking your life back*. As I was writing out these steps on a piece of paper, I felt emotional as I went through them, especially when I came to 'Taking your life back' because I know what that feels like and the joy that it has brought me. From nearly losing my own life to alcohol and drugs, I decided to take it back, and use it in a positive way rather than to destroy myself. That is really what this book has been about – *you* taking your life back and ceasing to destroy yourself with food. I'm asking you to hold your head up today and to feel good about yourself. Give yourself, not a second chance, but a first chance at getting well. I want you to give back that lifetime present called guilt. Give all the guilt back, it doesn't belong to you. It's a wasted emotion that you don't use today.

It's time for you to forgive yourself and break free from those chains and that obsession you have with food. To close the door on your old life and walk towards your freedom. You deserve all of this and I really hope that you will put the work into attaining it. It is possible if you will just follow these steps.

I wish you love and hope for the future. God bless.